# EASY
# PAPER
# PROJECTS

## 60
### CRAFTS YOU CAN WEAR, GIFT, USE AND ADMIRE

## MAGGY WOODLEY
#### CREATOR OF RED TED ART

PAGE STREET
PUBLISHING CO.

PAGE STREET
PUBLISHING CO.

First published in 2019 by

Page Street Publishing Co.

27 Congress Street, Suite 105

Salem, MA  01970

www.pagestreetpublishing.com

Distributed by Macmillan, sales in Canada by The Canadian Manda Group.

23    22    21    20    19      2    3    4    5

ISBN-13: 978-1-62414-850-7

ISBN-10: 1-62414-850-6

Library of Congress Control Number:  2018967515

Cover and book design by Laura Gallant for Page Street Publishing Co.

Photography by Maggy Woodley

Printed and bound in China

# DEDICATION

To Max & Pippa, may you always be crafty.

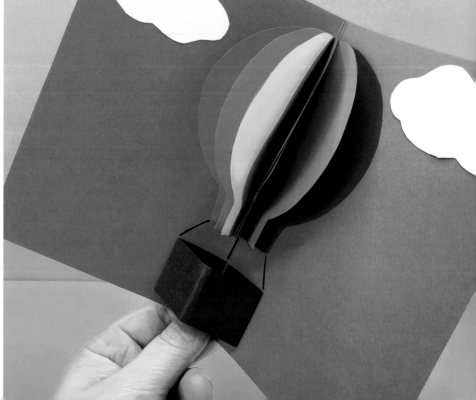

# TABLE OF CONTENTS

# INTRODUCTION

I am a strong believer that everyone can be creative. There are no rules to creativity, no right and wrong. I also believe that everyone can craft—especially if given the right creative guidance, support and materials. You can also nurture creativity and you can practice being creative. This book is all about finding your inner craftiness, gaining confidence when making and having fun!

I have been creating, writing and filming craft projects for over nine years on both my website (www.redtedart.com) and my YouTube channel (@redtedart). Over the years, I have learned a lot of about my readers and viewers—in particular, that:

1. Most people want to be creative.

2. Not everyone has the experience to get started.

3. Many "kids craft" projects online are far too difficult. (I can't even do them and it is my job to get crafty!)

4. Many people don't have access to the range of materials or specialist equipment to get started.

5. Many families don't have the space or time for messy or intricate projects.

I am passionate about overcoming these challenges and bringing the joy of crafting to all. The concept for this paper crafts book was born: Making crafting easy, fun, doable.

The majority of projects in this book are also nonmessy and quick, so that they can be done in smaller spaces and within a hectic family life.

Although this book creates fantastic projects out of paper, it is not an origami book (though we touch on origami here and there, to build on our paper-folding skills). Paper is like magic. With a little bit of practice and guidance, paper can be turned into so many cool craft projects. Let yourself be surprised by how versatile paper is. You will want to make them all!

The book gives you freedom (and hopefully encouragement) to make things your own way. For example, I show you a pop-up card (pages 74 and 78)—ask yourself how could you make it again but differently? I give you a gift box (page 126)—think of how you could decorate it to personalize it for the person you are giving it to.

Furthermore, this book uses the absolute minimum of materials (more information in The Materials section [page 8]). Essentially, you will need just paper and light card stock! Many paper craft books available on the market still require special items; e.g., a wooden bead in just the right size, a picture frame to decoupage. This book is unique in that the projects more or less use only paper. No extra items needed. Plus, they are fun, colorful, practical and can be gifted or kept. They are great for decorating your room or organizing your desk. Along the way you will be taught special paper-crafting techniques, which will allow you to come up with your own unique projects in the future. I give you a tool kit of paper-crafting skills to enjoy, experiment and have fun with!

So, are you ready to get started? Let's take a look and see what amazing things you can make using paper! Some things to note . . .

## WHO IS THIS BOOK FOR?

This book is for anyone that loves to craft, whether you are an expert crafter already, looking for some new ideas to try out or a little bit nervous about knowing where to start. There are range of projects—some super simple, easier ones (also great if you have less time) and some more complicated ones, if you want to challenge yourself.

The book assumes basic scissor-handling skills—younger readers may wish to work on these projects under the supervision of an adult.

## EMBRACE THE HANDMADE

One thing to remember about being creative and making things is to embrace the handmade. Handmade things are always *imperfectly perfect*! It is the imperfections that make them so special and unique. You are creating something that is lovingly handmade and that you can't buy anywhere else in the world.

Embrace the wonky line, adore that lopsided eye. Don't worry about a smudge here and there or a slightly lopsided craft. It makes your craft unique and special.

## MISTAKES HELP YOU LEARN

Also remember that we learn from our mistakes. Often, I use scrap paper to practice something first. Sometimes I make my own (scrap paper) templates. Sometimes I have a go at folding a new origami item with scrap paper first. This allows me to practice and to learn before I use my favorite new paper!

## THE MATERIALS

The ethos of this book is accessibility and thriftiness. By stocking up on some basic items, you should be able to make *all* of the projects in this book. All these items are inexpensive!

**1.** White and a rainbow-colored variety of printer paper

**2.** Some light card stock

**3.** Ribbons or baker's twine

**4.** Recycled items (including scrap paper for practice)

**5.** Basic office supplies—pens, scissors, a glue stick, a stapler and tape

**6.** Some sewing equipment—a needle and thread

In essence, paper, scissors and a glue stick . . . and you are ready to go!

## ABOUT PAPER AND LIGHT CARD STOCK

Paper comes in different weights and sizes. Most "printer-quality paper" is about 20 pounds (80 gsm) and 8½ x 11 inches (21.6 x 27.9 cm). Most of the projects in this book use this kind of paper.

If you can't obtain rainbow colors, you can still use this book, but improvise—maybe you can recycle some wrapping paper? Or decorate the crafts with pens instead of using colored paper?

We also use some light card stock—80 to 100 pound (120 to 150 gsm). This is perfect material for card making. It is sold in the same sheet dimensions as printer paper.

If you can't obtain light card stock, again improvise—can you upcycle an old greeting card and stick plain paper over the top? Can you stick two or even three sheets of plain paper together to make it stronger?

You will see that some projects call for 5½ x 8½-inch (14 x 21.6-cm) paper or stock, which is one-half of a full sheet. Similarly, 4¼ x 5½-inch (10.8 x 14-cm) paper or stock is one-quarter of a full sheet. Be sure to save whatever portions you don't use, to make more of the same or another project!

## BE THRIFTY

This book also encourages you to reuse and be thrifty with your paper. I have two large envelopes in my craft pile—one contains "medium paper scraps"; the other, "small paper scraps." I use both often!

You can replace some of the paper used here with brown kraft paper, too, to stay thrifty and use less of your colorful paper.

Always cut your shapes close to the edge of the paper to make the most of it! Then, pop any off cuts into your envelopes for reuse at a later time!

We also have a pile of scrap paper in our house. Scrap paper is great for practicing basic origami or folds, for cutting out your own templates or for practicing a bit of drawing.

In a few projects, I also use some printed paper—you can use recycled gift wrap for this instead.

## OTHER SUPPLIES

The tools in this book include:

1. Scissors
2. Glue stick (very important!)
3. Stapler
4. Tape
5. Ruler
6. PVA glue (white glue that dries clear)
7. Pencils
8. Pens (mainly black pens)
9. Safety pins
10. Paper clips

In addition, you may also need:

1. Ribbons or baker's twine
2. Needle and thread
3. Paper plates (see Notes)
4. Tin cans (see Notes)

**NOTES:** When I call for other materials—such as empty tin cans or paper plates—remember, you can always improvise. For example, where I use a paper plate, you can use cardboard from a cereal box or a delivery carton. Have a look at what is in your recycling box and see what you can use to craft with. Paper can turn something old into something new and magical!

Although not called for in this book, you can also add such items as googly eyes, stickers or washi tape to your crafts! Use what you have already and have fun!

Maggy Woodley

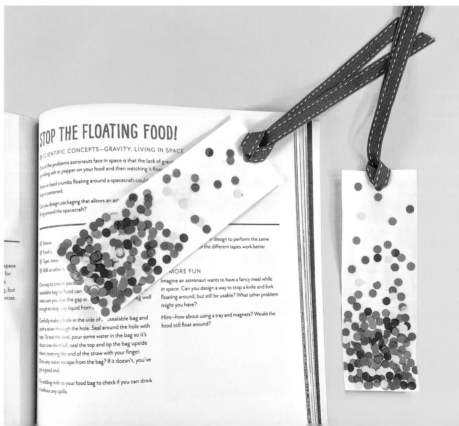

# CUTE & EASY BOOKMARKS

How a bookmark serves us well! Bookmarks are quick and easy to make and the perfect paper craft. I am always looking for my bookmarks . . . and so am in constant demand for new ones. They are great for inserting into books at school, marking pages you need to study and, of course, to keep your place in your latest read.

My family always gives books at birthdays and Christmas. Adding a personalized design makes the bookish gift extra special. Or pop a bookmark into a thank-you card to a teacher as a small gift. Finally, many a bookmark has been made and sold at school fairs! It's a great little fundraiser for schools or charities.

You will learn some basic origami skills, as well as how you can create a number of different cute designs and animals just using basic shapes, such as circles and ovals!

Once you have learned some basic bookmark designs and ideas, what else can you turn them into?

## CRAFTS IN THIS CHAPTER

# ORIGAMI CORNER BOOKMARKS

We love origami bookmarks and once you know how to make a basic bookmark, you can design hundreds of different ones.

Let's begin with the very basic corner bookmark and how you can quickly and easily decorate it. The next projects will share with you different ways to decorate your bookmarks even further!

## MATERIALS
- 1 square piece of paper (6" [15-cm] square is nice!)

## TOOLS
- Pens (optional)

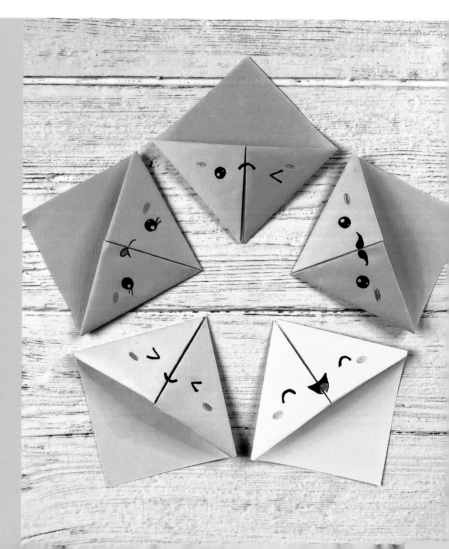

1. Rotate your square piece of paper so it is a diamond in front of you. Bring the lower point up to meet the top and make a neat crease across the center diagonal of your paper. You will now have a triangle.

2. Fold the lower right corner up to meet the top right angled corner.

3. Repeat for the left side.

4. Fold these 2 back open.

5. Flip down 1 of the top sheets and crease to create a triangle (see image).

6. Now, fold the flaps you created back up and tuck into your bookmark.

7. Repeat for the other side.

8. Congratulations—you have just created your basic origami bookmark!

9. Now, add some super cute and simple faces . . . and your first origami bookmark is done!

# CORNER BOOKMARKS
# PANDA & FRIENDS

Now that you have learned how to fold a basic origami bookmark, it is time to get your imagination into gear and turn the bookmarks into something special with some simple embellishments. Here we show you how to make a panda in detail, as well as the basic shapes needed to turn your bookmark into a penguin, owl or pig! They are just examples of how quickly and easily some basic shapes can transform your craft. What else can you make in this way? A monkey? A cow? A dog? Let your imagination run wild!

## MATERIALS
- Squares of paper, each about a 6" (15-cm) square
- Paper scraps

## TOOLS
- Scissors
- Glue stick
- Pens

## TOP TIPS
Let your added features overlap the edges of your bookmark. You can then trim them afterward to make them fit perfectly to the edge of your bookmark to finish it off.

## STEP 2 OPTIONS

**1.** Make your basic origami bookmark (page 12) in the color that you want your bookmark animal to be in—white for a panda, black for a penguin, any color for an owl (here we did one in purple) and pink for a pig!

**2.** Next, you will need to cut out your basic shapes that will transform your bookmark into your desired animal. What feature makes the animal *that* animal? What are the eyes like? What is the nose like? What are the ears like? Can we add additional features, such as paws and limbs? Here are the features for the panda and his friends.

**3.** Once you have your shapes, use a glue stick to glue down the facial features and add any necessary additional details with a black pen; e.g., your panda's nose, mouth and pupils. Continue to add any other features—in our case, the panda's black stripe, arms and legs.

Look at the image for the additional shapes needed for the panda bookmark's friends. Can you see how simple it is to transform your corner bookmark into a penguin, owl or pig? Now, over to you. What other animals can you think of?

It really is great to save your paper scraps as you go along! Today's penguin beak and feet are made from leftovers of our 3-D Pumpkin (page 152) in the Fall & Halloween chapter!

# KITTEN PAPER CLIP
# BOOKMARKS

These cute little paper clip bookmarks use basic shapes to create your adorable kitten characters. The shapes are the same for all three different kitten postures! Once you have the hang of these bookmarks, take these basic shapes and see what other cute animals you can create! What would you need to change to turn this into an adorable panda bear? Or a cute dragon? Your imagination is the limit!

## MATERIALS

- Light card stock or paper
- Paper clips

## TOOLS

- Scissors
- Lead pencil
- Glue stick
- Black pen
- Colored pencils
- Tape

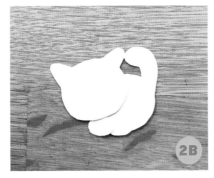

## STEP 2 OPTIONS

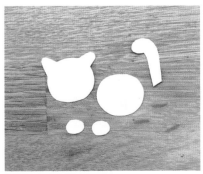

1. Draw and cut out 2 ovals (1¼ x ¾ inch [3 x 2 cm] is nice, but it is a question of preference). These 2 ovals will make the body and the head. The head is an oval with 2 additional triangles to make kitten ears. If you need help creating the right size ovals, lightly tracing around a coin or the lid of your glue stick with a lead pencil is a great way to start off, to achieve the right width—then sketch that circle into an oval and you have a basic template. You will also need a tail (think: umbrella handle) and 2 small ovals (⅜ x ¼ inch [1 cm x 5 mm]) for the paws.

2. By arranging the body parts differently, your kitten can be sitting, sleeping or in a playful mood! Once you're happy with your kitten's posture, use a glue stick to carefully glue the pieces into place. Now, add more details with a black pen and colored pencils. This is a great time to get creative and really bring your kittens to life and give them cute little characters!

3. Use tape to affix a paper clip to the back— remember to leave enough of the paper clip free to fit over the edge of your book page.

# CONFETTI BOOKMARKS

One thing I love to be is thrifty! As you know from this book, I always encourage you to make do with what you have, cut near the edges of a paper and above all, keep all your paper scraps! Because yes, you can get crafty even with the smallest of pieces of paper. Turn your paper scraps into colorful confetti and make some simple but gorgeous confetti bookmarks!

## MATERIALS

- Scraps of colorful paper
- White card stock (or paper stuck onto cardboard cut from a cereal box)*
- Ribbon (optional)
- Pompom attached to some yarn (optional)

  *You can make these bookmarks any size you want. My final bookmark is about 5½ x 1½" (14 x 4 cm), so I started with the corner of a larger piece of card stock that I later cut down.

## TOOLS

- Hole punch
- PVA glue
- Scissors

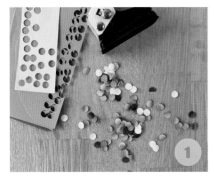

1. First of all, go wild and make lots of colorful confetti with your hole punch (be sure to catch it all in a bowl so it doesn't go everywhere), using your old paper scraps!

2. Take a piece of white card stock and add lots of PVA glue to it. If you don't have white card stock, stick white paper onto a piece of cardboard cut from a cereal box. Sprinkle on your confetti. If you wish, you can distribute the confetti bits evenly, *or* you can bunch them up at 1 end and have few at the other end, as if they are falling down your card and landing on the bottom.

3. Once you are happy with the layout of your confetti, add lots of PVA glue to the *top* of your confetti and carefully, using a finger, spread out the PVA glue. This creates a nice smooth layer over the top of your bookmark, a little like laminating. Do take care, though, and avoid folding or scrunching up any confetti. Make sure you get glue all the way up to the edges and beyond the confetti—so that you have a nice, even, shiny layer of glue across the whole bookmark.

4. Let dry fully. Once dry, your bookmark will be a little bendy as PVA glue has a tendency to curl paper. It is damp and that makes paper buckle. Don't worry—you can flatten it again later. Cut out a neat rectangle to make your bookmark— whatever size you prefer. I cut mine to 5½ x 1½ inches (14 x 4 cm). Again, it is a question of preference.

5. Hole punch a hole in the top and thread through some ribbon or a colorful pompom attached to some yarn! Put your bookmark inside some heavy books and allow it to flatten before gifting it to a friend!

# UNICORN
# "HUG A BOOK"
# BOOKMARK

It is time for a "Hug a Book" Bookmark. They are so cute and fun to make. I share step by step how to make a pandacorn, but at the back of the book you will find a template for both the pandacorn and a unicorn "hug a book." Although the templates are handy, I challenge you to have a go at creating the template yourself. What other creatures and characters can you make in this format? A fox? A bunny? Maybe Santa?

## MATERIALS

- Light card stock* in unicorn or pandacorn color
- Scrap paper for features, such as a muzzle, flowers and horn

*If you don't have light card stock, but only paper, use some recycled cardboard—such as from a cereal box—and glue your paper on! Or you can glue a couple of layers of paper together to make it stronger.

## TOOLS

- Lead pencil
- Scissors
- Glue stick
- Pens

1. Use a lead pencil and the template provided (page 180) to draw and cut your basic shapes from white card stock. You can also draw your own template. The main size of the unicorn bookmark is 6¼ x 1½ inches (16 x 4 cm). The pandacorn is the same width, but shorter.

2. Use the template to cut extra parts for your bookmark; e.g., for the pandacorn, use the body to outline the black feet; for the unicorn, trace the muzzle around the unicorn's head template. Also, draw and cut out some small flowers and leaves from your scrap paper, as well as a golden horn. If you don't have golden paper, improvise— use yellow or white, or maybe you have a gold pen? Cut out all the additional pieces.

3. With a glue stick, glue the front paws/hooves onto the top of the long piece of card stock— making sure you glue only the top bit of the paws/hooves, as you want the lower part to hang over the book. Then, start the layering of the remaining features: add the head and ears for the pandacorn, the head and muzzle for the unicorn. Add any final details in pen.

# TOO COOL FOR SCHOOL— GET ORGANIZED

Time to get your room ready for back to school! Let's get our desks organized and some basic stationery supplies in place.

Again, you will be honing your origami skills—you will love how quick and easy the little Paper Clip Boxes (page 24) are! Up your folding skills by making amazing Paper Pen Pots (page 30)! Or learn how easy it is to upcycle a tin can and make a cute desk tidy (one of my favorite five-minute makes!).

Create some fun mini notebooks—either a pullout version in the form of a rainbow cloud, or mini notebooks from one sheet of paper—always popular with my kids.

## CRAFTS IN THIS CHAPTER

# PAPER
# CLIP BOX

Super simple and fun paper boxes to help keep your desk or drawers tidy. We like to keep paper clips and cute erasers in ours; what will you put in yours? They are a great way to color coordinate your desk accessories. I chose rainbow colors for mine, but you can go monochrome or use pretty patterned paper!

## MATERIALS

- Per tray: 3 pieces of square paper (3¼" [8.5-cm] square is nice, but it is a question of preference!)

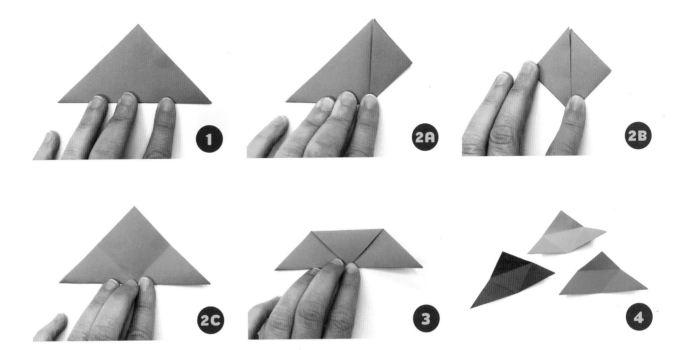

1. Place a square piece of paper in front of you like a diamond and bring the bottom corner up to meet the top corner.

2. Bring the bottom right corner up to meet the top corner, creating a perpendicular line down the middle. Repeat with the bottom left corner. Once completed, you should have a new, smaller diamond with an opening that opens running down the middle. Open up this opening to show your triangle again.

3. Bring the top 2 points of paper forward and down—making the top corner meet the center of the horizontal fold at the bottom. Then, fold open again. You should now have a triangle with folds running across it that create 4 smaller triangles.

4. Repeat with your second and third pieces of paper.

(continued)

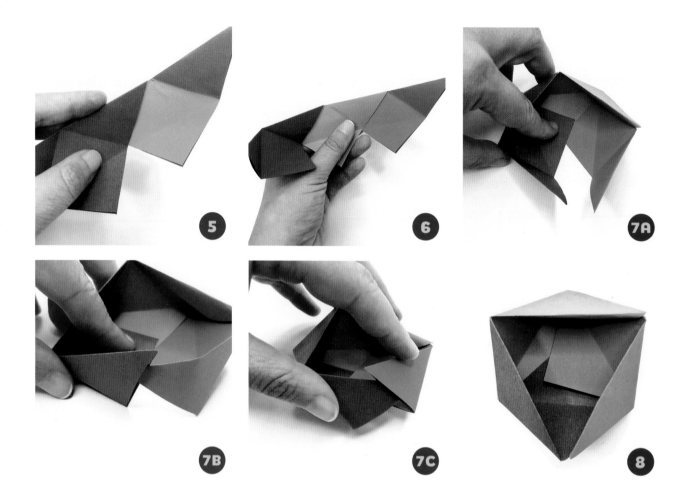

# PAPER CLIP BOX (CONT.)

**5.** Take 1 of your triangles—make the large 90-degree corner point down—so your horizontal part of the triangle is parallel to your work surface. Take a second triangle in the same way and insert the pointy left corner (at a 45-degree angle) into the right-hand pointy corner of the first.

**6.** Take the third triangle and insert into the second triangle in the same way. Your 3 pieces should now be connected—a long horizontal running across the top and three 90-degree points pointing down.

**7.** To bring it all together, take the right-hand point of the third triangle and insert it into the left-hand point of the first triangle—so now all 3 sheets of paper are connected end to end.

**8.** While doing so, push the central pieces of paper together to create a base for your box. If you wish, you can finish this off by adding a little glue to the base sheets of paper to strengthen the box, but this shouldn't be necessary.

# TIN CAN
# PEN POTS

This is a great five-minute craft to decorate your room or desk with some colorful Tin Can Pen Pots. It is amazing how just a little bit of paper can transform your "waste" and create something useful and new in minutes. Learn how to make the basic tin can decoration and then experiment and see what else you can make—can you turn our "cute faces" into a penguin or watermelon? What other designs can you come up with? Old pieces of wrapping paper are great for this, too!

## MATERIALS
- Empty, clean tin cans
- Paper in desired colors, large enough to go completely around your can

## TOOLS
- Ruler
- Scissors
- Pens or paper scraps, for decorating
- Tape

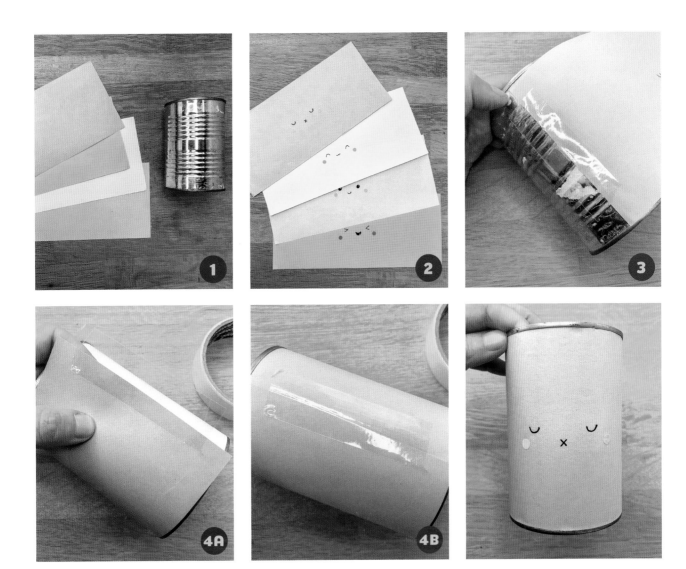

1. Remove as much paper from your tin can as possible. If a little glue remains on the can, that is fine; you won't see it. Measure out your paper by wrapping it around the can to see how long and wide it needs to be. Cut out the correct size. In our example, that is 9¾ x 4 inches (25 x 10 cm).

2. Decorate your paper, making sure your decorations are in the *center* of your paper and remembering that the paper will curve around the sides. That is, most decorations should be in the middle 2 to 2¾ inches (5 to 7 cm) of your paper.

3. To secure the paper to your tin can, you simply add a strip of tape along the short edge of 1 side of the paper. Position this paper with the tape vertical along the back of the can, then press the tape down.

4. Wrap the paper as neatly as possible around the can. Secure the second edge of the paper with a second piece of tape to finish making your pencil holder.

# PAPER
## PEN POTS

These pen pots are so fun to make and look great! They are good enough to give as gifts, too! At first they will look complicated, but take your time and you will see that they are really easy to make! As with the paper clip holders (page 24), you can choose colors to suit your own decor or color theme! Again, patterned paper would look fabulous, too. Or make it in plain white for that chic sophisticated look!

## MATERIALS
- 6 sheets of printer paper, each about 8½" (21.6-cm) square
- Smaller paper scraps, to add contrasting colors
- A little light card stock or recycled cardboard, for the base

## TOOLS
- Glue stick
- PVA glue
- Scissors

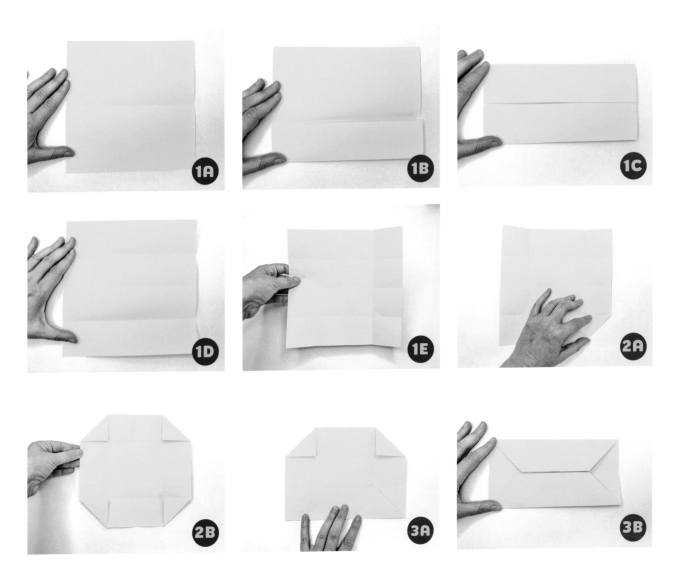

1. To make your first segment, you will need to begin by folding your paper into a 4 x 4 square grid. To do this, fold the paper in half, then open it up and fold the top and bottom of the paper in toward the central fold. Open it up fully, turn your paper 90 degrees and repeat. When you unfold your sheet of paper, you should have 3 folds running across and 3 folds running down your paper—creating 4 x 4 squares.

2. Take the bottom right corner and fold it into a small triangle that sits neatly within the bottom right square. Repeat for all 4 corners.

3. Take the bottom edge (with triangles folded in on either end) and fold, so the edge meets the central line. Repeat with the top half.

(continued)

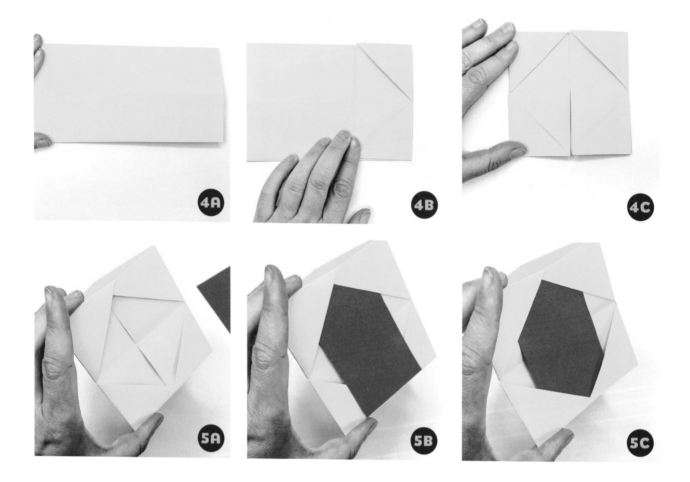

# PAPER PEN POTS (CONT.)

**4.** Turn your paper over. Using your folds as guidelines, fold the paper from the right into the center. And repeat for the left side.

**5.** This is now the magical part! Insert the right side of the paper into the left side ever so slightly—this will start to turn your flat shape into a 3-D triangular prism that you need at the end. Add your contrasting piece of paper into the square you can see.

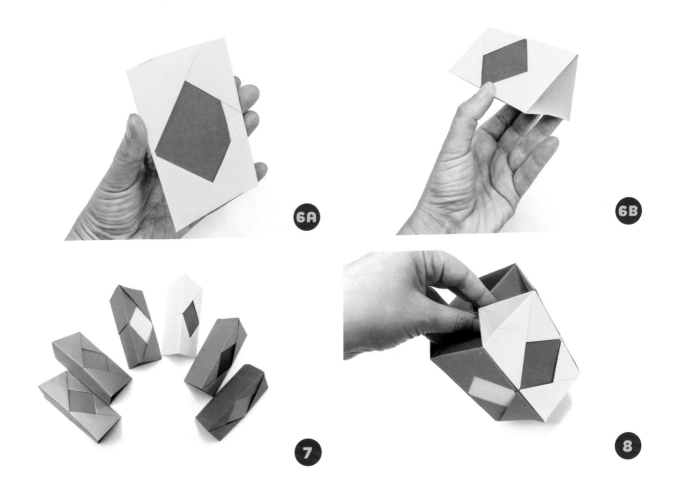

6. Keep squeezing the left and right edges gently together, carefully nudging the shape into place to create the triangular prism. Your first part of your paper pen pot is finished.

7. Repeat 5 times, using contrasting colors if you wish.

8. To assemble: Using a glue stick, glue the 6 parts together as neatly as possible. Use PVA glue to glue the base onto some card stock large enough to extend beyond the sides and let dry. Once dry, trim the base to the shape of your paper pencil pot. You can now fill your pencil holder with pens and pencils!

# BADGER
# NOTEBOOK

Once you have learned how to make this fun mini notebook, you can make them in endless designs! You only need one sheet of paper to make two mini notebooks, and should you decide to decorate only with pens, this can be made with no glue! Hooray!

## MATERIALS
- 1 sheet of printer paper or A4 paper
- Colored paper scraps (optional)

## TOOLS
- Scissors
- Pens
- Glue stick (optional)

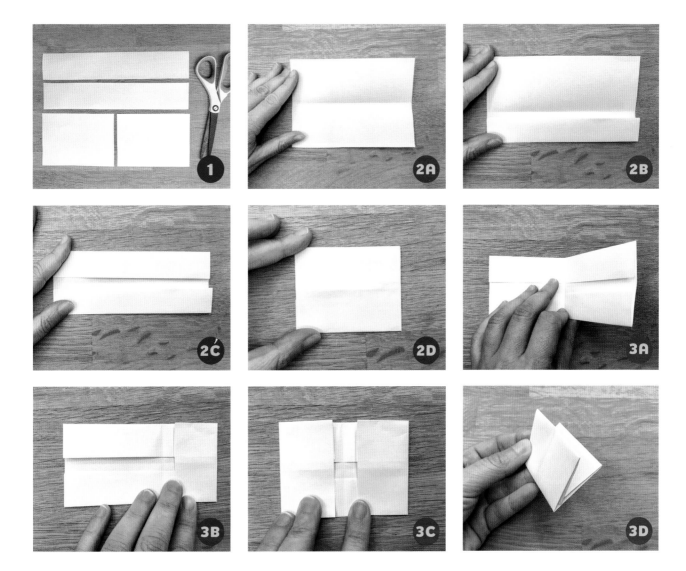

## MAKE YOUR COVER

1. Fold your sheet of paper lengthwise and cut in half. Take 1 of these halves and cut it in half *widthwise*. Cut the other strip in half *lengthwise*. You should have 4 sheets of paper—2 (4¼ x 5½-inch [10.8 x 14-cm]) squarish rectangles and 2 (2⅛ x 11-inch [5.4 x 27.9-cm]) strips; these are approximate sizes. Set aside 1 rectangle and 1 strip to use to make a second notebook, or add those pieces to your scrap paper stash.

2. Take the squarish rectangle and *lightly* crease it lengthwise. Open it up. Bring the bottom edge of the paper to just *below* the central crease, ¼ inch (5 mm) away from the edge. Repeat with the top half.

3. Now, fold the same piece of paper in half across its width, creating a fold that will be the spine of your notebook. Open it up. Fold the right side toward the central fold but ¼ inch (5 mm) short of it. Repeat for the left side. You have now created the book jacket cover for your notebook.

(continued)

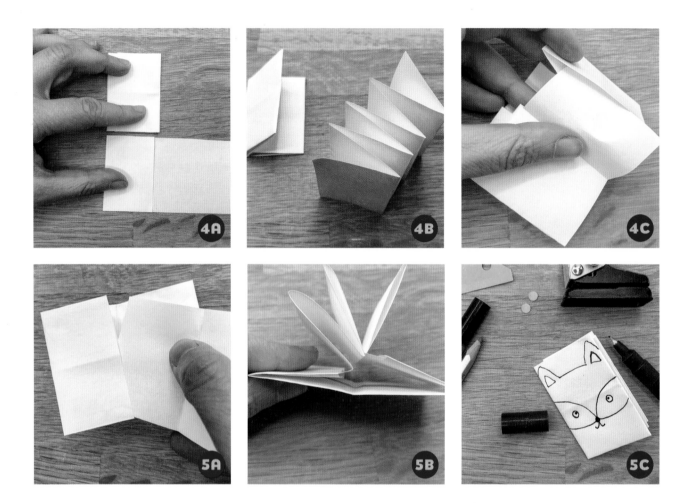

# BADGER NOTEBOOK (CONT.)

## MAKE YOUR PAGES

**4.** Take the long, thin strip and measure it against your notebook cover. Make sure your first fold is slightly narrower than the notebook cover. Accordion-fold the rest of the paper to fit inside the cover. If you find there is a little bit left over at the end, trim this off.

## ASSEMBLE YOUR NOTEBOOK

**5.** Insert the accordion-folded paper into the cover of your mini notebook. The basic notebook is now finished! Decorate with pens and/or use a glue stick to add paper! What will you turn your mini notebook into? It can have animals on it, or you can add some cool 3-D letters.

# CLOUD
# NOTEBOOK

A super fun and colorful notebook to make for back to school. These notebooks could also be used as greeting cards! Choose your favorite colors or make them in rainbow colors. Or use the same technique and, instead of clouds, create something new—maybe an apple? A heart? A flower? What else could you make as a cover?

## MATERIALS

- Square sheets of paper, about 3" (7.5-cm) square, in rainbow colors—an uneven number is best
- White paper or card stock for the clouds
- Scraps of pink or purple paper (the final color in the rainbow)

## TOOLS

- Ruler
- Scissors
- Pens
- Glue stick

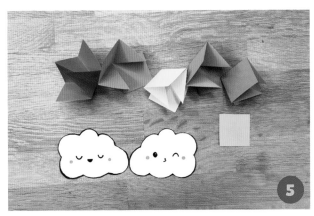

1. To create a rainbow, you need to make some guideline folds on your square pieces of paper. Fold each square in half to make a rectangle. Open up and fold again in the other direction. When you open it up, the folds should divide it into 4 equal squares.

2. Flip the paper over. Take the bottom right-hand corner and fold to meet the top left corner, creating a triangle. Open again and you should now be able to see a new folded diagonal. Flip the paper over again.

3. The next bit is a little tricky. Put your left index finger on the center of the page where all the folds meet and, with your right hand, push the diagonal crease inward. Repeat with the left-hand side, so that the diagonal crease folds back up again and meets in the center. When fully folded, you will have a smaller square again, with tucked in sides.

4. Repeat with the remaining 4 colors, so that you have 5 colors in total.

5. Cut out a 1½-inch (4-cm) square piece of pink paper to complete the rainbow, as well as 2 white clouds that you can use a pen to decorate with cute faces, which will completely cover your squares when folded.

(continued)

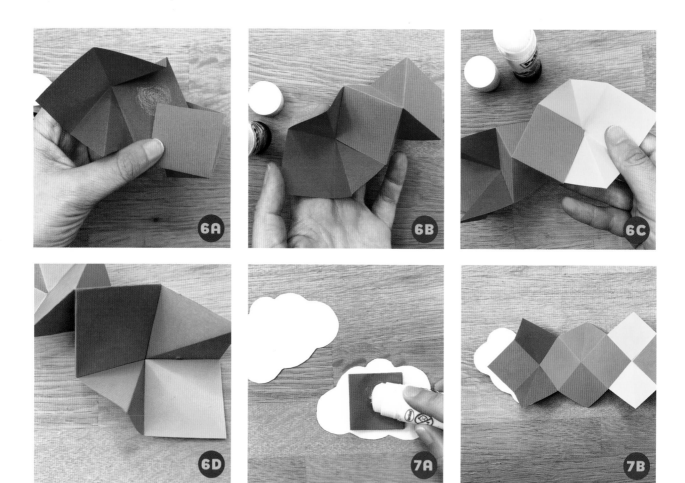

# CLOUD NOTEBOOK (CONT.)

**6.** Assemble your rainbow pullout by lining up your rainbow colors, flipping every second square over. They will be glued together in reverse. Using a glue stick, add glue to 1 corner, then glue the second color, facing downward, onto the first corner. Repeat, alternating the squares facing up or down. Add your little pink square at the end.

**7.** Glue your rainbow pullout onto your cloud covers to finish off your notebook.

# ARTY PAPER
## LUMINARIES

These arty paper lanterns are one of our favorite makes for colder, darker days as fall and winter approach. They make cozy little nightlights or decorations for the mantel piece and can be adapted for all seasons and themes. The luminaries are super quick and easy to make. They look fabulous and celebrate the inner artist—a marvelous way to have a go at doodling. There are no real rights or wrongs, and as with many crafts in this book, only your imagination is the limit!

## MATERIALS
- White printer paper or A4 paper
- Battery-powered tea light

## TOOLS
- Scissors
- Pens
- Glue stick, tape or stapler

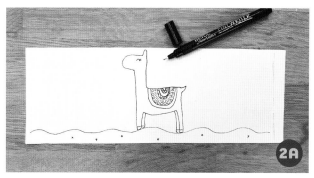

1. Cut your piece of printer paper in half lengthwise, so that you end up with 2 rectangles, each 4¼ x 11 inches (10.8 x 27.9 cm) long; this is an approximate measure. Set 1 strip aside to make a second lantern or add it to your scrap paper stash.

2. Doodle away with pens. I like to start in the center of the page because it is likely to be the main part of the luminary that you will see. You can do it in just black and white or use colors, too! *Do* leave a ⅜-inch (1-cm) strip of white at 1 edge of your paper for gluing later.

3. Optional: Cut out the outline of the top of your doodling, to give the luminary some shape. The light will also reflect nicely. But you can skip this step, if you wish.

4. Roll the paper into a cylinder (with the drawing on the outside) and secure the ends with a glue stick or tape or staples. Place on the table and pop your tea light inside.

# WEAR YOUR CRAFTS

So, your room is back-to-school ready! How about you? Want to make some last-minute accessories or gifts for friends?

Making things you can wear or give to friends is a great way to get crafty, and paper once again, can be turned into fabulous DIY jewelry. As with all of this book, the materials are kept simple, but if you have jewelry-making kits at home, you can upscale the ideas in this chapter to your heart's desire!

In this chapter, you will learn how to make simple bracelets, brooches and bow ties! You can adapt your paper crafts for many situations. For example, the Paper Bow Tie (page 58) can be worn as a tie or as a hair accessory, or used when card making or for decorating gifts. Similarly, the layered Flower Brooch (page 52) is a great way to use up a range of paper scraps and can be worn as a brooch or hair accessory or used for decorating cards and gifts.

In this chapter, we focus on our paper-folding skills when making lucky stars and bow ties, as well as on our quilling skills for the Cloud Brooch (page 54). What other designs could you come up with?

## CRAFTS IN THIS CHAPTER

# ORIGAMI
# LUCKY STARS BRACELET

Wish upon a lucky star! These origami lucky stars at first feel tricky, but once you get the hang of them, you will be making them over and over, with any scraps of paper you can find. Here, I turn them into adorable little lucky star bracelets to make for friends, or you can incorporate them into other craft projects, such as my Quilled Christmas Tree Card (page 82): pop an origami star at the top! So cute.

## MATERIALS

- Strips of paper, ⅜" to ⅝" (1 to 1.5 cm) wide and 11" (27.9 cm) long (from the long edge of printer paper or A4 paper)
- Optional: beads (if making a bracelet)
- Elastic thread

## TOOLS

- Ruler
- Scissors
- Needle (with a wide eye to fit the elastic through)
- Pens (optional)

### TOP TIP

Add a coat of PVA glue to the stars and let dry. This will stiffen the paper and make it stronger.

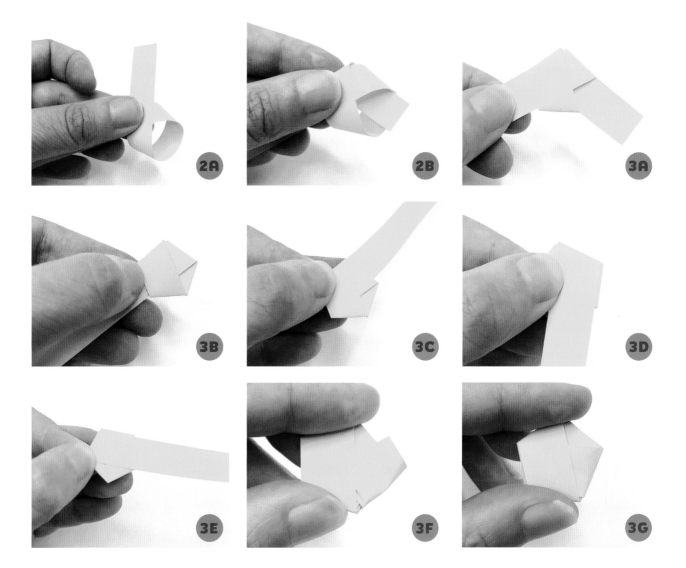

1. Each strip of paper will make 1 star. Try to cut it as neatly as possible. You can make the strip thinner or wider depending on how big you want your star to be; ⅜ of an inch (1 cm) wide seems like a good size!

## TO MAKE A STAR

2. Fold the paper over on itself to create a loop. Next, push the short end of the paper through this loop, as if making a knot! In fact, you *are* making a knot . . . but with paper instead of string. Tighten the knot carefully and flatten.

3. Fold this little flap over—backward or forward; it doesn't matter, so long as it's flat against the edge of the knot. If it overlaps the sides a little, you can trim with scissors or tear. You should now have a pentagon shape. Now, take the long strip of paper and, always flattening it against the edge of the pentagon, wrap it around itself. Repeat until you come to the end of the paper. Then, take the last little flap and tuck it under the last fold. You should now have a fully formed pentagon with no pieces sticking out.

(continued)

# ORIGAMI LUCKY STARS (CONT.)

4. Now comes the trickiest bit and sometimes it doesn't work. If it doesn't, don't worry; just try it again. It will get easier. Take your pentagon and hold it between both thumbs and index fingers. Pinch on 1 side. Then, go around the pentagon until you have pinched in all the sides and you have a little star.

5. These little stars look great on their own (maybe write a wish on the paper before folding into a star), but would also look adorable as part of a paper ornament or added to a 3-D card craft! Decorate with pens to make a face.

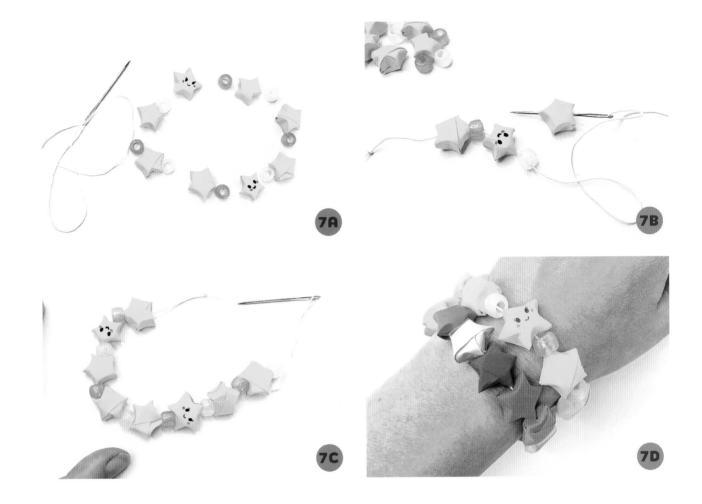

7A

7B

7C

7D

## TO MAKE A BRACELET

**6.** Depending on size of the bracelet you wish to make, make 8 to 12 paper stars.

> **NOTE:** You may want to ask an adult to help you with this step!

**7.** Thread your elastic through your needle. It needs to be a sharp needle, or else you won't be able to thread the stars. Thread the stars alternating with beads, if you wish. If you don't have any beads, make more stars and use only the stars! Tie the ends of your elastic together and your lucky star bracelet is ready for wearing.

# QUICK
# PAPER BRACELET

This is a super quick and fun craft that you can make for yourself or a friend. They are so easy that you can make lots for all your friends. Once you have worked out how to fold these, you can make them out of any scrap of paper—magazines, newspapers and so on.

## MATERIALS
- Squares of paper, 6″ (15-cm) square, in two colors*

## TOOLS
- Ruler
- Glue stick or tape (optional)

*This paper bracelet looks the best in two colors. Origami paper, which is usually white on one side and colored or patterned on the other, is best for this. But plain paper is fine, too. Scraps of old birthday or Christmas gift wrap is perfect for this also! Alternatively, you can use a glue stick to glue two sheets of paper together, but that will make a thicker bracelet

6″ (15 cm) square is a good size for a child's bracelet. For an adult, use a bigger square.

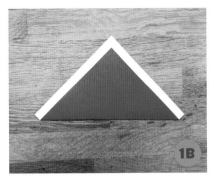

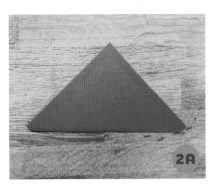

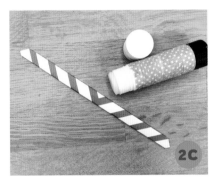

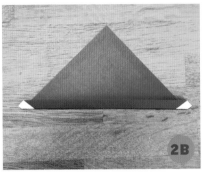

1. Turn your paper so that the white side is facing up and you have a diamond. Bring the bottom corner up and fold it toward the top corner. Instead of making a perfect triangle, fold so that the bottom point is about ⅜ inch (1 cm) below the top point, creating a white outline.

2. Flip your paper over. Make a ⅜-inch (1-cm) fold upward along the bottom long side of the triangle. Continue to fold until you reach the top. Secure with a little glue, if you wish. You should have a striped strip of paper.

3. Gently fold the paper strip to bring the 2 ends together and make a ring shape. Then, slot 1 end into the other. Finished! You can secure it with a little glue or tape, if you wish.

# FLOWER BROOCH

These layered paper flowers can be used in lots of different ways. Our favorite is to wear them as a brooch; however, you can add them to a barrette, make a set of them and wear them as a necklace by gluing them onto a piece of cardboard and attaching that to ribbons or decorate gifts and greeting cards with them.

## MATERIALS
- Circles of paper in different colors
- Safety pin

## TOOLS
- Lead pencil or compass
- Ruler
- Round objects to trace (optional)
- Scissors
- Glue stick
- Tape

## TOP TIP
You can glue a layer of cardboard, from a cereal box, to the back of the flower brooch to strengthen it before adding the safety pin. Be sure to cut it small enough not to show from the front of the flower.

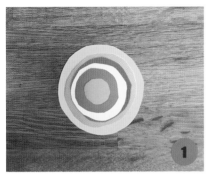

1. Use a lead pencil to draw 6 circles in difference sizes. Use a compass if you need help with this. Alternatively, find lots of differently sized round things to trace, from tin cans to bottle lids and coins! Our largest circle is about 2¾ inches (7 cm) in diameter, the smallest is about 1 inch (2.5 cm) in diameter. When layered up, they should all fit inside each other! Cut out your circles.

2. Stick the smallest circle into the center of the second smallest. Cut petals or frills into the second smallest and fold upward to give them more dimension. Take the third smallest and make a light outline of where the center section will go. Cut out some petals around this outline. Fold the petals upward and use a glue stick to glue into place. Repeat this step with the next size circle, and so on. Mix up your petals, making some round, some pointy, or cut some straight lines. Remember: They don't need to be perfect to look great!

3. Once the final layer has been added, tape a safety pin to the back and you are done.

What ways can you think of to use this paper flower?

# CLOUD
# BROOCH

This brooch is supereasy to make and a great way to use paper scraps. It hones your paper quilling skills that will also be used in the paper quilled cards (page 82). The cloud is a great first brooch project as you can use simple white printer paper and some colorful paper scraps. I challenge you think of other designs you could make using this technique. Maybe make a paper quilled balloon? Or maybe a simple heart?

## MATERIALS

- White paper at least 6" (15 cm) long
- Paper scraps in rainbow colors
- An old birthday card or cardboard from a cereal box (or several layers of paper glued together)
- Safety pin

## TOOLS

- Ruler
- Scissors
- Paper cutter (optional)
- Toothpick or knitting needle or fingers
- Glue stick
- PVA glue
- Tape

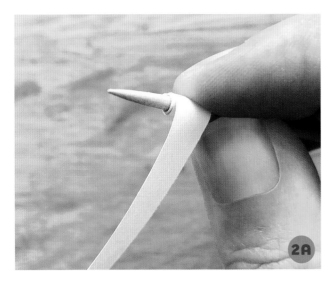

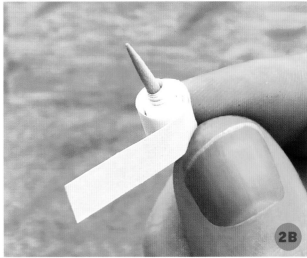

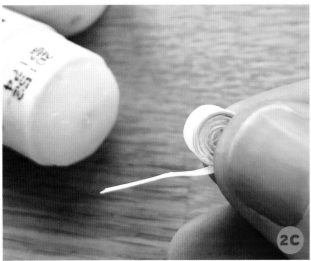

1. To make the cloud coils, you will begin by cutting a number of white paper strips. Cut them as evenly as possible and not too wide; a paper cutter might come in handy here. I cut strips roughly ¼ inch (5 mm) wide and 4 to 6 inches (10 to 15 cm) long. The different lengths will give you differently sized curls.

2. Curl the end of your paper around a toothpick or knitting needle and roll it up fully. You can do this just using your hands, but it is a little fiddlier and can be hard to roll small! When you have a quill of the desired size (you can relax your grip on it a little to loosen the quill and make it bigger), secure with a glue stick. Repeat and make a number of white paper quills in different sizes.

(continued)

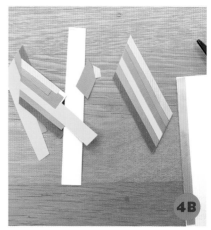

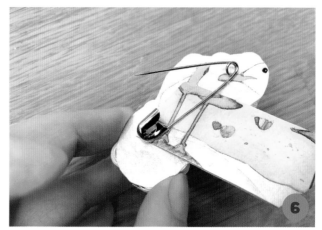

# CLOUD BROOCH (CONT.)

**3.** Cut out a cloud shape from you recycled card and, using PVA glue, position your paper quills on the cloud. Try to keep to the shape of the cloud and fill it as neatly as possible.

**4.** To make the rainbow, cut some paper strips ⅜ inch (1 cm) wide in rainbow colors and attach them in this order: red, orange, yellow, green, blue and purple (or pink!). Using the glue stick, add a thin line of glue along 1 long edge of the red strip, then overlay with the next color, and so on. Cut the rainbow strip to your desired shape and glue 1 end to the back of your cloud.

**5.** Your basic quilled cloud is finished! If you wish, cut out small paper strips to add cute facial features to your cloud!

**6.** Finally, secure your safety pin (make sure it is the right away around) to the back of the cloud, with a little tape.

## TOP TIP

When it comes to paper jewelry, you can always add a layer of thin PVA glue, watered down a little, as a "varnish" over the entire front of the piece, which will strengthen it.

# PAPER<br/>BOW TIE

A superfun and easy bow tie that you can actually wear! This is a great edition to any fancy dress activity, or make it small and use as a hair bow. Make a simple black one for that smart look. Or a fun polka-dotted one for that quirky look. These would also look great as part of any card-making or present-decorating activities! Make them plain. Or turn them into fun animals.

## MATERIALS
- 1 sheet of white or colored printer paper or A4 paper

## TOOLS
- Ruler
- Scissors
- Tape
- Glue (optional)
- Pens (optional)
- Elastic or hair pin for wearing

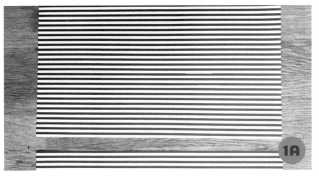

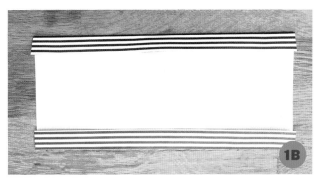

1. Begin by cutting a 1¼-inch (3-cm) strip of paper from along the full length of your sheet of paper and set it aside. Turn the remaining paper and fold in the long sides by ¾ inch (2 cm)—this doesn't need to be exact!—to give you a nice neat and strong edge.

2. Fold 1 short side of the paper to approximately the middle. Fold in the other side. You can overlap this with the right side and trim if desired. The resulting width at this stage will be the width of your bow tie, so you may want it a little smaller! I trimmed it back by ¾ to 1¼ inches (2 to 3 cm).

3. With the folds running perpendicular down the center, start accordion-folding your paper. You want to make 7 neat folds, creating 8 equally spaced-out sides. If you are having trouble with getting the folds equally spaced, you can make some "marker lines" by folding the paper in half first and thus finding the central fold.

(continued)

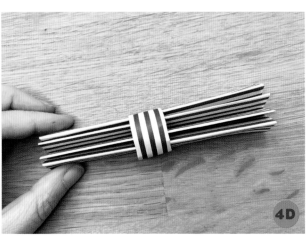

# PAPER BOW TIE (CONT.)

**4.** To make the center part of your bow, take your reserved strip of paper and trim it down to 3 x 1¼ inches (7.5 x 3 cm) wide. Fold in the long edges. Loop the strip over on itself to form a cylinder and tape in place. The loop should be about as big as you want your bow tie knot to look. Don't make it too loose. Push the accordion-folded paper through the middle.

**5.** Using your fingers, spread out the bow at both ends, while creasing the folds down near the bow tie knot to help keep it in place. You can add a little glue underneath the central part of the bow tie to secure it.

**6.** Finally, and this is optional, you can add some fun faces to your bow tie! As with many of the quirky characters in this book, stick to basic shapes—circles for eyes, triangles for ears, and so on. Be inspired by other characters in this book to decorate to your heart's content.

**7.** Thread some elastic through the back of the bow tie or attach a hair pin by running it through the back of the paper loop.

# PAPER PENDANTS

Yes, you can make paper pendants that you can wear! These are super fun and you can create them in all sorts of designs to suit your mood and outfits. Do note that this is a craft of patience! Each pendant doesn't take long to make, but you do need to leave longer drying times between steps. So, make sure you have somewhere to leave your work while it dries without your cat sitting on it or a sibling touching it!

## MATERIALS
- Scraps of white paper
- String, leather band or chain, for wearing

## TOOLS
- Black and colored waterproof pens (Sharpies preferred)
- Ruler
- Scissors
- Glue stick
- Strong PVA glue
- Toothpick (optional)

## TOP TIP

If you wish, you can use jump rings to hang these paper pendants. They look superneat and tidy and are nice and strong. However, we show you a great alternative here.

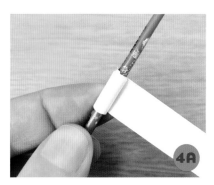

1. Use the pens to draw some pendant designs 1¼ to 2 inches (3 to 5 cm) high. Keep the outlines of your designs simple, so they are easier to cut out later. Outline with a black pen to make them pop! Be sure your pen marks are fully dry before moving on!

2. Cut out your design, leaving a little bit of margin to trim later, and glue onto 3 to 4 further layers with small pieces of paper, to make the pendant stiffer. A glue stick is good for this, as it will dry quickly. You want every piece to stick down neatly and well.

3. Add a generous layer of PVA glue on top to seal the design. You can use a toothpick to gently spread the glue to all the edges. Be careful; *some* pens will react to the glue and smudge. Sharpie brand pens work really well or substituting color photocopies of your work do, too.

4. While that is drying, cut a strip of paper about ¼ inch (5 mm) wide and 4 inches (10 cm) long. Rub the glue stick along 1 long edge and roll it up—leaving a gap in the middle of the cylinder wide enough for your string, leather band or chain to pass through. Rolling around a thin paintbrush handle or a knitting needle is often a good size.

5. Once the front of your pendant has fully dried, cut it out. Leave a thin margin of white around any fragile or detailed parts so they don't bend and break. Flip over and glue the paper cylinder to the back of it, near the top. Again, add a good layer of PVA glue all over the back, to seal the back of your pendant, but also to secure your hanging mechanism.

Once fully dry, your pendant is ready for wearing! Make some for your friends.

# BEST CARDS TO SURPRISE YOUR FRIENDS WITH

We love crafts that you can make and give! Sometimes, receiving a paper card in the mail brightens someone's day. Other times, you may want to say thank you to the best teacher. Or maybe you want to congratulate someone on a birthday or wedding day! A handmade card makes whatever you have to say extra special.

This chapter provides you with a basic card-making tool kit. You will learn how to make a basic pop-up card and use it with any design, about paper quilling and to make simple animal-shaped cards! Once you have mastered how to make these cards, you can adapt them to suit any card-giving situation as well as customize them to suit people's favorite colors or designs.

## CRAFTS IN THIS CHAPTER

# WEDDING
# CAKE CARD

Pop-up cards are so fun to make and surprisingly easy. This pop-up cake card can be customized for birthdays, anniversaries or weddings. Use scraps of paper, fabric or simply pens to decorate and personalize. Remember, think about the people you are giving this to: What colors do they love? What themes do they get excited about? Personalize it to suit them!

## MATERIALS

- ½ piece of white printer paper or A5 paper

- 1 piece of card stock, 5½ x 8½" (14 x 21.6 cm) or a ready-made folded greeting card that is 4¼ x 5½" (10.8 x 14 cm)

- Scraps of colored paper or lace

## TOOLS

- Ruler

- Scissors

- Glue stick

- Pens (optional)

- Hole punch (optional)

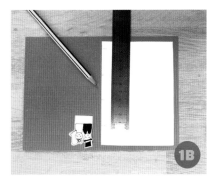

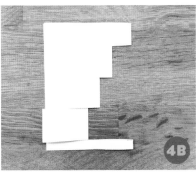

1. Using your card stock as a guide, cut down your sheet of white paper a little: ⅜ inch (1 cm) off the top and ⅜ inch (1 cm) off 1 side—so that when it is inside the card stock, you will have a nice frame that will work out to be about ¼ inch (5 mm) wide. Fold the white paper in half to fit into the card stock.

2. Think about your cake toppers: Will they be candles or a little bride and groom? Keep it simple; the result will look great and you don't have to be an artist to create details. I drew a small bride and groom and cut them out.

3. When you have prepared your cake toppers, line them up with your folded paper and roughly measure the length from the top of cake to the bottom of the cake. Divide this cake space into 3 equal-height "layers" along the spine.

4. The bottom layer of the cake should be approximately half the width of the card (in this case, about 2¾ inches [7 cm]). Make 4 cuts: 2 long cuts (each ¼ inch [5 mm]), 1 medium cut (1⅜ inches [3.5 cm]) and 1 small cut (¾ inch [2 cm]). To make the cake pop forward, you will now need to make a crease along these cuts. Fold open the paper and reverse the crease!

(continued)

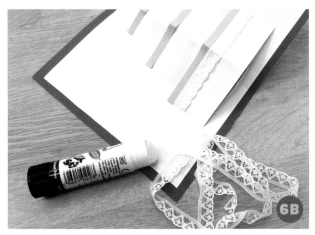

# WEDDING CAKE CARD (CONT.)

**5.** Using a glue stick, glue the cake into your card stock, 1 side at a time, pressing down to secure. Your basic pop-up cake is finished!

**6.** It is now time to decorate to your heart's content. In these examples, I decided to combine pink paper scraps with lace and a bride and groom drawing to make a wedding cake! But you can also use pretty patterned paper to make birthday cake layers and candles.

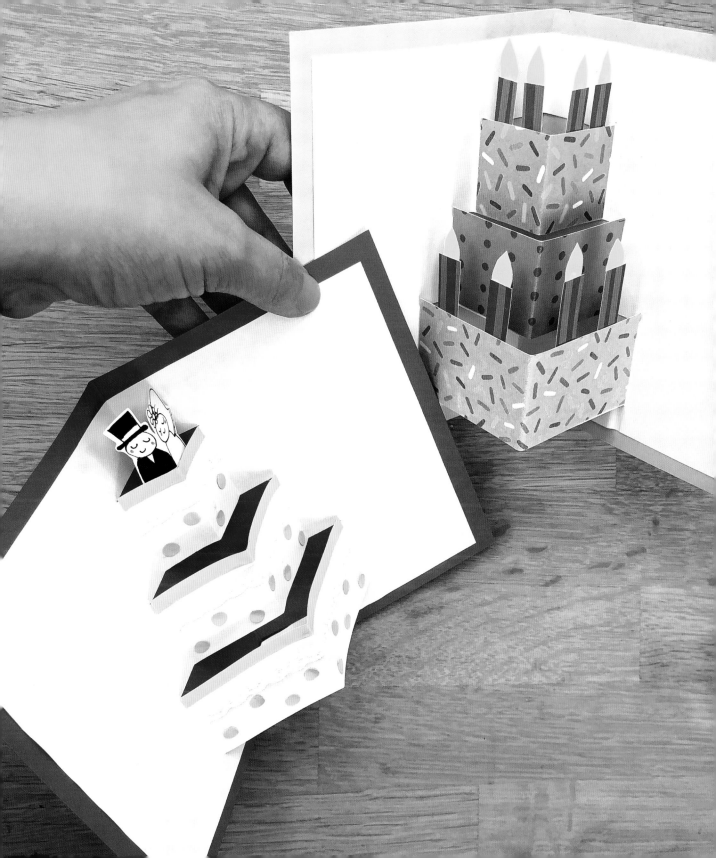

# LLAMA CARDS

I do love a llama craft. These easy cards use basic shapes for you to learn how to make on your very own from scratch. They make great cards to send through the mail (the head can detach, if you wish), but also make a super cute llama decoration.

## MATERIALS

- White card stock, 5½ x 8½" (14 x 21.6 cm)
- White card stock scraps
- White paper scraps

## TOOLS

- Lead pencil
- Ruler
- Scissors
- Pens
- Glue stick or tape
- Something circular for tracing; e.g., a large glass

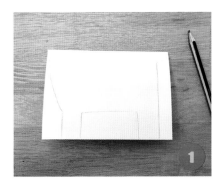

1. Begin by making a llama body from the card stock. Fold your white card stock in half. Using a lead pencil, mark out the basic shape of a llama. The easiest way to do this is to make a mark ¾ inch (2 cm) from the edge (beginning of the first leg), another ¾ inch (2 cm) along (end of the first leg), 1½ inches (4 cm) along (beginning of the second leg) and another ¾ inch (2 cm) farther along (end of the second leg). Make connecting lines upward—1 in a curve for the neck, 2 lines for the tummy and finally a straight line at the end, leaving space for the tail! You have drawn the basic outline of a llama body!

2. Now, cut out and shape the card into the llama's body, creating the tummy, 2 legs and a little tail. Trim a little more at the bottom of the legs to shape the hooves, leaving a ¼-inch (5-mm) square as a hoof shape.

3. To make the llama's neck and head, you can use the leftover pieces of card stock or extra pieces, if you want to make the head bigger. Using a lead pencil, sketch a curved top on a rectangle for the llama's head, and cut out. Also cut out 2 almost teardrop-shaped ears. Add facial details and ear details with pen, then glue all the pieces together with a glue stick.

(continued)

# LLAMA CARDS (CONT.)

**4.** Assemble your llama. Cut ¾ inch (2 cm) into the head at the bottom of the llama's neck, and cut a ⅜-inch (1-cm) slot into the card. Slide in the neck. You can secure the neck to the body with a little glue or tape on the inside of the card, if you wish.

**5.** To make the llama's blanket, use a lead pencil to draw a large circle on a scrap of white paper (e.g., use a wide glass—ours had a diameter of about 4 inches [10 cm]). Fold the circle in half and trim down the sides by about ⅜ inch (1 cm) on each side. When the blanket is opened up again, you should have an oblong or slightly more oval shape. Decorate with pens to your heart's content. To keep things even, it's easier to start on the outside and work your way in.

**6.** Once finished, fold the blanket in half and glue onto the llama's back. Add any finishing touches to resemble tassels and harnesses to the llama's neck and you are done!

# NEW HOME CARD
## BASIC POP-UP

Here you will learn how to make a basic pop-up card. In this instance, we have made a "new home" card, but you can use this concept for any occasion. Instead of a house and tree, make a fairy and gift pop-up for a "magical birthday." Or maybe draw a snowman and a Christmas tree for Christmas. Or maybe you want to cut out a photo of yourself and add it?
One simple technique, endless possibilities to get arty!

## MATERIALS
- ½ sheet of printer paper or A5 paper, in desired color
- Card stock, 5½ x 8½" (14 x 21.6 cm) or a ready-made folded greeting card that is 4¼ x 5½" (10.8 x 14 cm)
- Paper scraps for drawing and decorating

## TOOLS
- Ruler
- Scissors
- Lead pencil
- Pens (optional)
- Glue stick

1. Using your card stock as a guide, cut your sheet of white paper down a little: ⅜ inch (1 cm) off the top and ⅜ inch (1 cm) off 1 side—so that when it is inside the card, you will have a nice frame that will work out to be about ¼ inch (5 mm) wide. Fold the paper in half widthwise.

2. Using a lead pencil, mark 2 (⅜-inch [1-cm]) strips and 2 (¾-inch [2-cm]) strips along 1 side of your folded paper and then cut along the marks. In the example, I position the cuts as following: cut the first ¾-inch (2-cm) strip at 1¼ inches (3 cm) from the edge, and the second ¾-inch (2-cm) strip at 1½ inches (4 cm) from the edge. Then, make the first ⅜-inch (1-cm) cut at about 4 inches (10 cm) and the second ⅜-inch (1-cm) cut at about 4¼ inches (10.8 cm). This is where your pop-up designs will go. Fold the strips to create a crease. Then, push through to the other side and reverse the creases. This creates your pop-up tabs.

3. If you wish, shape 1 side of your paper. In this new home card, we cut a curve to create a rolling hill. But you can also leave it whole and decorate with pens! Glue the paper into place, using a glue stick.

4. Create some drawings around the theme of your card. Make sure they are not too big and that they fit the width of your card, including the indentation. For example, if your folded card is 2¾ inches (7 cm) wide and their distance from the central fold will be ¾ inch (2 cm), your drawing has to be under 2 inches (5 cm) high. Once you have checked their size, cut out your drawings and glue them onto the pop-up tabs.

5. Finish off the card by adding any additional details you wish, such as clouds in the sky or a path.

Now you have learned how to make a basic pop-up card, what else can you make pop up? See the flower garden (instead of 2 pop-ups, we used 5 pop-ups) and snowman example for more ideas!

# ICE CREAM POP CARD

I love to find things to reuse and recycle. The next time you eat an ice-cream pop, be sure to wash the stick and use it for this craft. Don't worry; you can use paper or cardboard instead if don't have any sticks. These cards are great for Valentine's Day—"you are so sweet," or for a birthday—"you are so cool" or any occasion you can think of!

## MATERIALS

- Light card stock, about 4¾" (12-cm) square
- Paper scraps, in contrasting colors, for decorating
- Washed and dried popsicle sticks or more card stock

## TOOLS

- Lead pencil
- Scissors
- Glue stick
- Pens

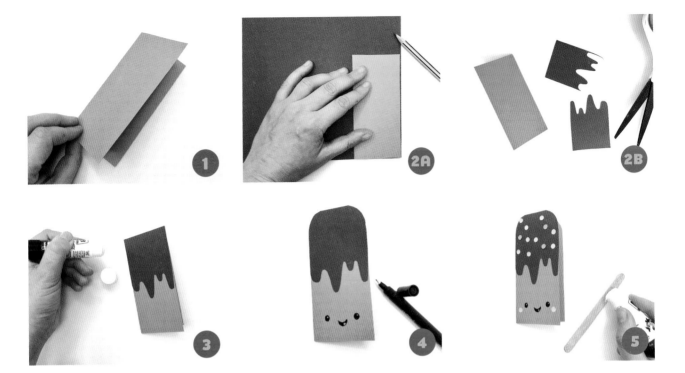

1. Begin by folding your card stock in half for your basic ice-cream pop shape.

2. To make the contrasting colors, using a lead pencil, trace the card onto your contrasting paper for the perfect size/fit. Then, cut out these shapes, adding a wiggly edge for a dripping ice cream effect, or dividing the colors to create different flavors.

3. Using a glue stick, glue onto your main card, then round off the edges at the top to give it that "ice pop shape."

4. Time to add those finishing touches. Draw on a cute face! Have fun and experiment with different expressions. Add some confetti sprinkles made from scrap paper.

5. At the very end, don't forget to glue on the stick!

What other ice-cream pop shapes and colors could you use? What other cute faces could you draw? Remember to embrace the imperfect—lines do not have to be 100 percent straight and glasses can be wonky!

# POP-UP
# HOT AIR
# BALLOON CARD

More fun with rainbows in the sky. Let's make one of these darling cards. You can make it as a rainbow, or in the recipient's favorite colors. Or maybe you have some pretty patterned paper that would look simply perfect. Another lovely birthday or good wishes card to someone going away on travels!

## MATERIALS

- A rainbow selection of paper scraps
- 1 piece of blue card stock, 5½ x 8½" (14 x 21.6 cm)
- Brown paper scraps
- White paper scraps

## TOOLS

- Lead pencil
- Something circular for tracing; e.g., a glass
- Scissors
- Glue stick
- Pens (optional)
- Ruler

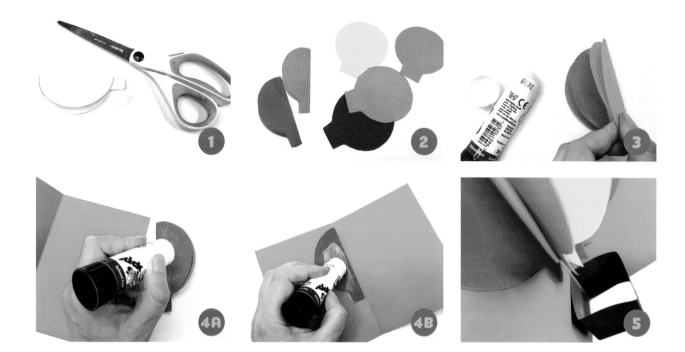

1. Begin by making your own hot-air balloon template: Using a lead pencil, trace something round (e.g., a glass) and add a little rectangle to the bottom. You need to have this symmetrical, so fold your template in half and trim off any excess, if needed.

2. Now, use your template to trace and cut out 5 or 6 hot-air balloon shapes in your desired colors. We chose 6 shapes to make the colors of the rainbow. If you choose 5, you could add a birthday number to the center of your hot-air balloon.

3. Fold in half vertically, making sure the rectangle at the bottom is aligned. Using a glue stick, add glue to 1 side of the red hot-air balloon and then stick 1 side of the orange balloon on top. Add glue to the second side of the orange balloon and add the yellow one and so on, until they are all stuck together. If you have decided to add a birthday number, place this third in line; that is, in the middle of your hot-air balloon.

4. Get your card stock ready. We like using a blue card as it represents the sky, but any color is fine. Add glue to the remaining red side of your hot-air balloon and position on your card. Then, repeat with the remaining colored balloon at the far side, gluing it to the other side of the card. Close the card and press down to secure it!

5. Make a little basket from a brown strip of paper; about 1 x 5 inches (2.5 x 13 cm) is great. Fold in half and fold in the flaps to create a little 3-D box shape. Glue down the flaps on either side of the card. Finally, add the hot-air balloon rope lines with a pen and cut out white paper clouds. Of course, you can add happy cute faces to the clouds, if you wish!

# PENNANT BANNER
## GIFT AND CARD

Ran out of wrapping paper but need to wrap a gift in a hurry? Want a matching card? Making a paper pennant banner is quick and easy and looks great on either brown kraft paper or white printer paper.

## MATERIALS
- Paper scraps in different colors
- Baker's twine, string or thin ribbon

## TOOLS
- Ruler
- Scissors
- Tape (optional)
- Glue stick

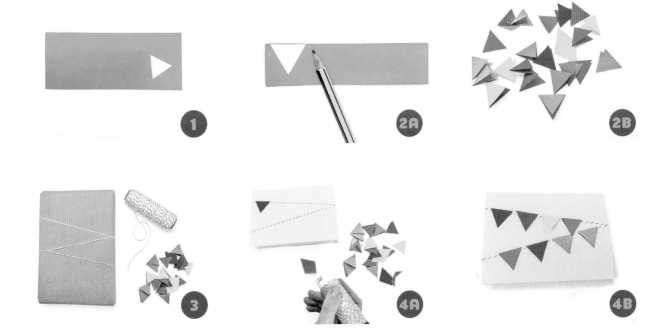

1. To make things neat and even, begin by making yourself a little triangular template: a triangle ¾ inch (2 cm) wide and high is good.

2. Now, cut your banner triangles. Begin by folding a piece of your colorful paper in half lengthwise and placing 1 edge the triangle template across the folded edge. Trace and cut. When opened, you should have a double triangle with a center fold. Repeat in lots of colors.

3. Time to decorate your card and gift. Wrap your baker's twine 2 or 3 times around your card and gift. Secure at the back with a knot. If you wish, you can also tape it in place at the back to prevent it from slipping.

4. Open up your triangles, use the glue stick to add a little glue, refold the triangles over your baker's twine and glue in place. Repeat until you have filled in all the baker's twine. In my case, that was 8 paper triangles for the card and 13 for the gift!

# QUILLED
# CHRISTMAS TREE CARD

Paper quilling is a great paper-crafting technique to learn about and get into. This project uses a very basic version of this traditional craft. You can use this technique to create designs for any occasion—here, we use it to make Christmas tree cards!

## MATERIALS

- Green, red, brown and yellow paper
- 1 piece of card stock, 5½ x 8½" (14 x 21.6 cm) or a ready-made folded greeting card that is 4¼ x 5½" (10.8 x 14 cm)

## TOOLS

- Ruler
- Scissors
- Toothpick or knitting needle or fingers
- PVA glue

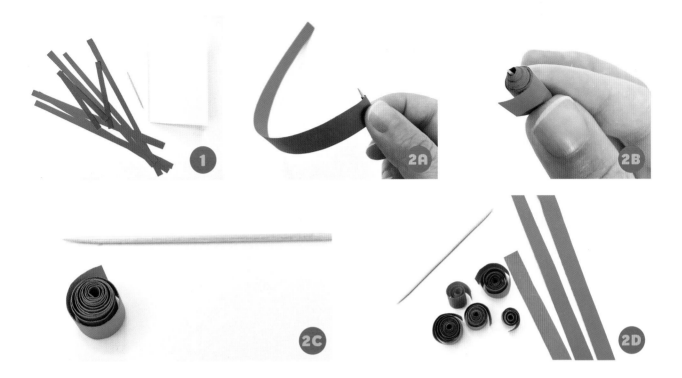

1. Cut strips of colored paper along the long edge of a piece of paper, cutting them about ⅜ inch (1 cm) wide. Make them different lengths; for example, 8½- and 11-inches (21.6- and 27.9-cm) long strips. Being sure to reserve 1 long strip of green paper for the tree outline, cut other strips in different greens (if you have more than 1 green) and some in red (to be used as ornaments; other colors welcomed, too!).

2. Except for the reserved long strip of green, coil the green strips tightly around a toothpick or knitting needle. They will stay coiled when you remove them. Alternatively, use your fingers to carefully roll them up as tightly as you can.

3. Now, you can either prepare the tree shape ahead of the crafting session and let it dry fully—this will result in a beautifully triangular Christmas tree shape—or you can skip the drying process and proceed. However, the latter risks resulting in slightly wonky trees. We love the wonky trees as it personalizes each tree. However, this really is a matter of personal preference!

(continued)

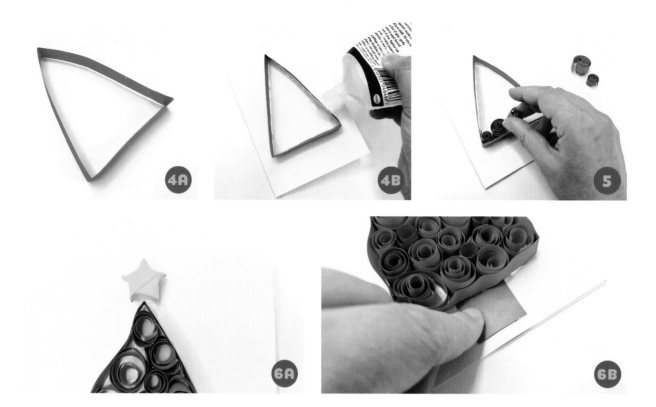

# QUILLED CHRISTMAS TREE CARD (CONT.)

**4.** Fold along your long strip of green paper at roughly 4 inches (10 cm), at 4 inches (10 cm) farther along and then at about 2¾ inches (7 cm)—leaving ⅜ inch (1 cm) at the end. It is not an exact measure. These folds will form the sides of your Christmas tree triangle. Using PVA glue, glue the ⅜-inch (1-cm) fold to the top of the first 4-inch (10-cm) section = triangle made. Now, run some glue along the edges and position on the front of the folded card, leaving space for a small trunk below and a little star at the top.

**5.** Time to add your paper coils. Fill the inside of your tree with glue and start arranging your green coils on the glue. Once it is more or less full, make some little red coils and fill the gaps as if they were little red Christmas tree ornaments.

**6.** As a finishing touch, you can either add a yellow paper star cut from 2 triangles or make an origami lucky star (page 46)! You will also need to cut a brown rectangle for the trunk and glue into place.

If you enjoy this technique, why not have a go at creating other designs of your own? For example, a heart filled in with paper quills would look amazing for a Valentine's or Mother's Day Card!

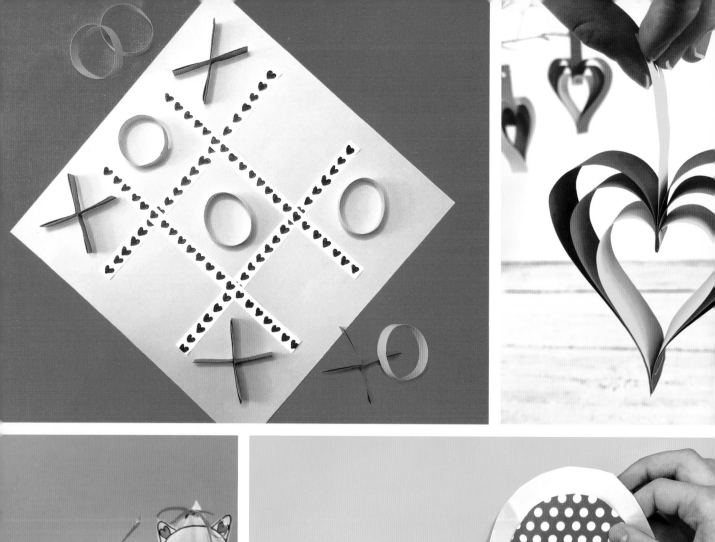

# SAY IT WITH LOVE

We do love to craft. Especially for such occasions as Valentine's or Mother's Day. Don't worry, this chapter isn't all pinks and reds (though you are more than welcome to use these traditional "love colors")—you can create these "love-inspired" paper crafts all year round.

In this chapter are both decorating ideas (e.g., gorgeous Paper Strip Hearts [page 88]; they look amazing and are surprisingly quick and easy to make) and gift ideas (how cute are the Animal Boxes [page 92]?). We will be developing some of our paper-folding accuracy with the Nested Heart Envelopes (page 98), as well as make use of the paper fan technique—using same shapes glued together for a 3-D effect—when making our cute Heart Notebooks (page 90)!

## CRAFTS IN THIS CHAPTER

# PAPER STRIP
# HEARTS

A super simple heart decoration that you can make in any color combination. These look great as individual hearts hanging in an ornamental tree, or you can string them up as a paper heart garland or hang them as a heart mobile. Super versatile, so easy!

## MATERIALS
- 11" (27.9-cm)-long paper, in 3 different colors
- Paper strip scraps, for hanging

## TOOLS
- Lead pencil
- Ruler
- Scissors
- Stapler
- Hole punch

## TOP TIP
The paper hanger can replaced by ribbon or baker's twine, if you wish!

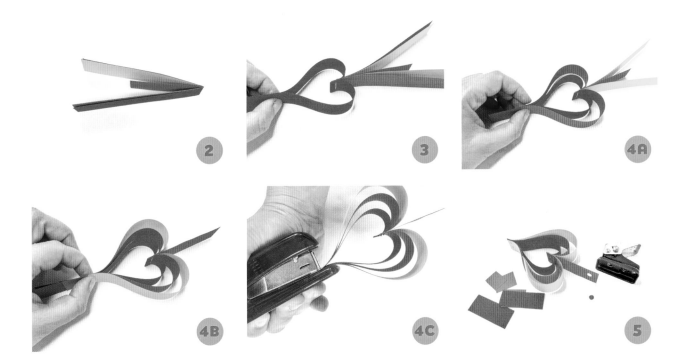

1. Using a lead pencil, mark 2 strips of 1 color paper to about ⅜ x 11 inches (1 x 27.9 cm), a third strip of the same size from your second color and 1 smaller strip about ⅜ x 2⅜ inches (1 x 6 cm) from either color, and cut them out.

2. Place the 3 long strips together and fold in half. The color on the inside of the fold will be the color of your heart on the outside once finished. Place your small strip on the inside of the fold, too. Now, secure at the bottom of the fold with a staple.

3. Holding the stapled part of your heart and with your paper strips point up, fold down the 2 outside strips and hold in place.

4. Then, without letting go of the first 2 strips, take the next 2 strips (second color) and again fold down—this time bringing them ¾ inch (2 cm) along from the bottom of first 2 strips. Hold in place. Now, take the final 2 strips and fold down, again about ¾ inch (2 cm) along from the bottom color. Make sure they are all neatly aligned—each strip of paper with its partner. Staple in place.

5. You can now trim the bottom. Also, trim the 2⅜-inch (6-cm) strip at the center to a length that you like for hanging and add a hole for hanging with a hole punch.

# HEART
# NOTEBOOK

A sweet little heart notebook for Valentine's Day or just because! These colorful notebooks are quick and easy to make!

## MATERIALS
- Paper in different colors
- White paper or card stock

## TOOLS
- Lead pencil
- Scissors
- Glue stick
- Ruler (optional)
- Pens (optional)

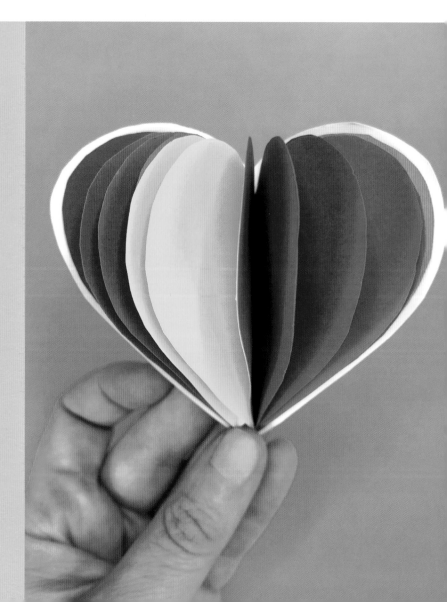

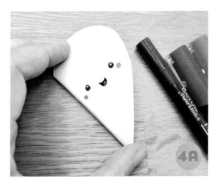

1. Make a heart template or trace the heart in the back of the book (page 183). Then, tracing around the template with a lead pencil, cut out as many hearts as you would like to have in your notebook. We decided to cut 2 of each of the rainbow colors.

2. Fold each heart in half. Use a glue stick to add glue to 1 side of the first heart and stick it to 1 side of the second heart. Repeat until all the hearts are glued together.

3. Glue onto a piece of white paper or lightweight white card stock. Cut the paper to shape— maybe leaving about ¼ inch (5 mm) around to make a little white frame.

4. Now, if you wish, you can use pens to decorate the cover, by adding a cute face to the outside of your heart!

# ANIMAL BOX
# FOR VALENTINES

Learn how to make this easy pyramid box that uses a basic square! Once you have learned how to make these fabulous little treat boxes, you can decorate them for all seasons. We share some Valentine's designs with some fun puns for you here. But think how else you could decorate these—maybe for Mother's Day or a friend's birthday?

## MATERIALS
- 1 sheet of paper paper or light card stock
- Ribbon, for tying

## TOOLS
- Ruler
- Lead pencil
- Scissors
- Hole punch
- Pens
- Glue stick

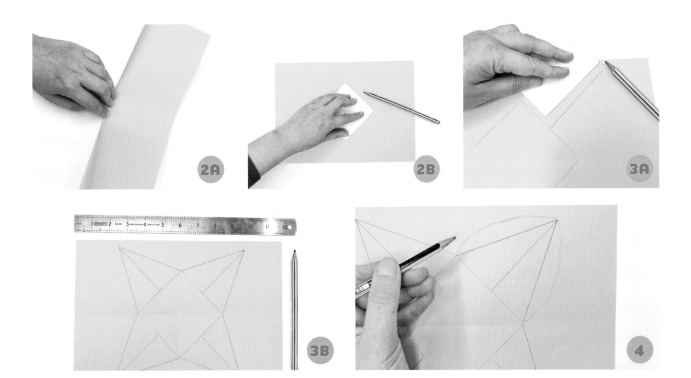

1. Make yourself a perfect square template—3¼-inches (8.5-cm) square is a nice size, but the pyramids can be bigger or smaller. Be as accurate as you can so that the template is perfectly square. Fold in half and use a lead pencil to mark this central fold of the square; you will need it later.

2. Fold your sheet of paper in half widthwise and lightly crease it down the middle. Open and repeat lengthwise. This gives you the center of the paper. Place your square template at a diagonal into the center of the paper and trace it with the pencil.

3. Use the square template again, this time aligning it along 1 edge of the drawn square, fold it in half and draw a pencil line along it onto the paper. Repeat until you have done this to all 4 sides of the main square. Draw a line from the corners of the main square to the tip of the line—to create 4 triangles on the outside of the square.

4. This next bit doesn't have to be super neat: Use the pencil to draw a curve going from the top of each triangle to the main square. These will be the flaps of your box.

(continued)

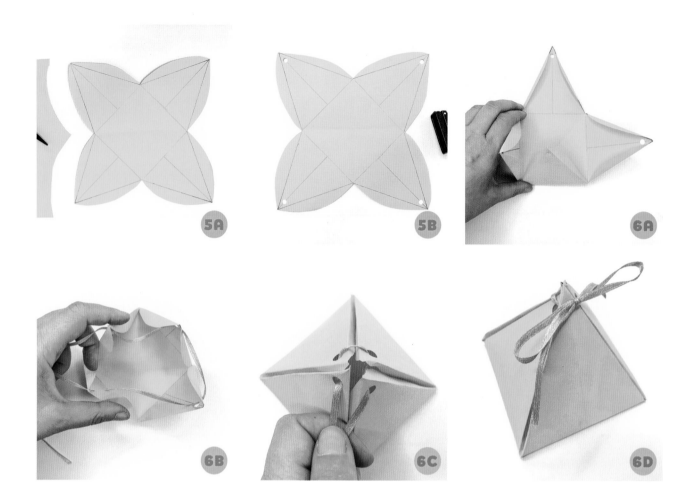

# ANIMAL BOX
# FOR VALENTINES (CONT.)

**5.** Now, cut out the entire shape as neatly as you can—keep the leftover pieces of paper for your decorations. Make a hole at the top of each triangle with a hole punch.

**6.** Make neat creases along the edge of the square and triangles. Fold in. Weave a ribbon through the 4 holes: Feed the ribbon through the outside of the first hole, push the ribbon back out through the inside of the second triangle out, bring it back inside through the outside of the third hole and finally weave the ribbon through the fourth hole, going from the inside out. If you thread the ribbon this way, you will get a nice neat closure and place to make your bow.

8A

8B

8C

8D

**7.** Time to decorate! Here I made a cat and a bear. However, you can decorate your box whichever way you want. Flick through this book for inspiration for other animals and other holidays or seasons!

**8.** Sketch out your cat or bear face, and once you're happy with it, redraw it in black pen. If you need to, trace around something round and add ears. Cut out the head, some paws and a mouth; then a heart on which to write your Valentine's Day pun ("You're the Beary Best" or "You Are Pawsome"). Use a glue stick to glue in place.

What other puns can you think of and what other animals can you design?

# HUGS & KISSES
## GAME

Instead of sending a Valentine's Day card, why not make your BFF or loved one a "Hugs & Kisses" game? Ever noticed how tic-tac-toe is made up of kisses (X) and hugs (O)? This makes the perfect little DIY Valentine's Day paper craft!

## MATERIALS

- 1 sheet of printer paper, for base
- White paper at least 7" (17.8-cm) long, for grid
- 2 sheets of printer paper, in contrasting colors, for hugs and kisses

## TOOLS

- Ruler
- Scissors
- Lead pencil
- Pens (optional)
- Glue stick

## HOW TO PLAY TIC-TAC-TOE

The aim of the game is to get 3 of your own pieces in a row. Players take turns to place 1 marker. Block the path of your opponent while trying to create your own row of 3.

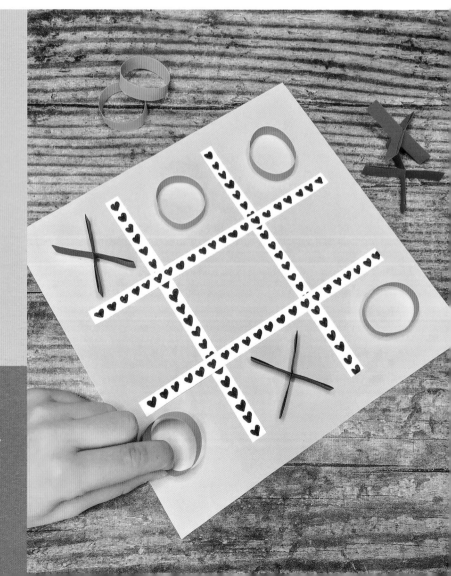

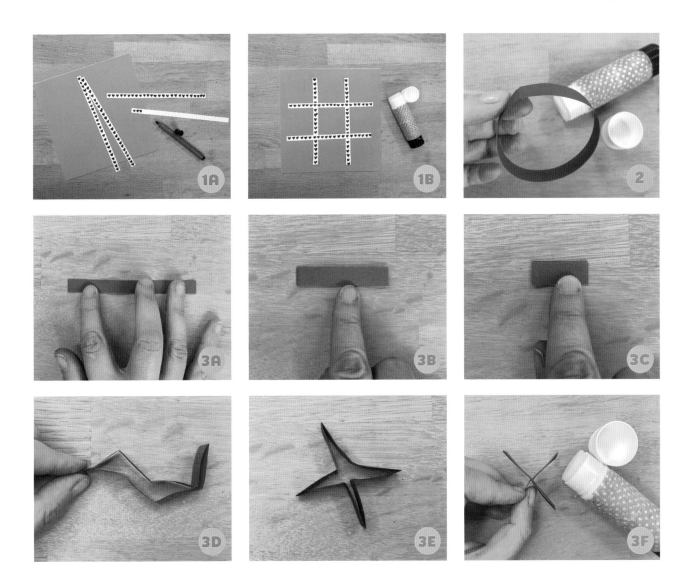

1. Cut your sheet of paper into a square (about 8½-inch [21.6-cm] square) to make the base of your game. Next, use a lead pencil to mark out 4 (7 x ⅜-inch [17.7 x 1-cm]) strips of white paper, cut out and decorate with hearts (or anything else!). Using a glue stick, glue these onto the square sheet of paper to form a 2 x 2 grid.

2. To make a hug, cut a ⅜ x 4-inch (1 x 10-cm) strip of colored paper. Add a little glue to 1 end and bring the ends together to make a loop (an *O*). Repeat until you have 5 hugs of the same color.

3. To make a kiss, cut a ⅜ x 8-inch (1 x 20.3-cm) strip from a different color of paper. Glue together to make a loop. Flatten the loop, then fold in half and in half again. You should end up with a piece of paper folded 8 times and glued together at the ends. Accordion-fold the folds so that you have 1 going in and 1 going out—until you end up with a star shape. Add a little glue to the inside and press together to form your kiss (an *X*). Make a total of 5 kisses.

# NESTED HEART
# ENVELOPES

We love these heart envelopes, as they are quick to make and introduce you to the art of origami (and folding neat lines!). Once you get the hang of these, you won't stop making them!

## MATERIALS
- Paper in different colors or designs

## TOOLS
- Lead pencil
- Scissors
- Ruler
- Pens, for adding messages
- Glue

1. Use the heart templates at the back of this book (page 183).

2. Fold a piece of paper in half, make a neat crease and align the heart template the spine of the fold. Trace with a lead pencil and cut out your heart. Repeat to make hearts in the 3 different sizes!

3. Open 1 heart. You will see that you have a neat crease down the center of it. Fold over half of the heart but not perfectly—it must overlap this central crease by ¼ to ⅜ inch (5 mm to 1 cm). The crease you are creating must be in parallel to the center crease.

4. Repeat from the other side, this time making sure you overlap symmetrically. Where the 2 heart folds meet, should be the center of your heart. Fold down the top of your heart.

5. Fold up the bottom of your heart—enough so that it neatly overlaps the top flaps. Then insert into the top flaps. Your first heart envelope is finished.

6. Repeat with the other 2 heart sizes.

7. Now, open up all your hearts again and glue them inside one another. Refold. Embellish with any messages of love!

# SCRAPS
# HEART ORNAMENT

These paper scrap hearts are super fun to make and look oh so pretty. They can be used to decorate your wall, turn into a greeting card or even to create a little paper heart bag!

## MATERIALS

- 2 sheets of printer paper, in contrasting colors
- Paper scraps in various colors, cut into ⅜" (1-cm) strips
- Ribbon or baker's twine, for hanging

## TOOLS

- Lead pencil
- Scissors
- Glue stick
- Hole punch

## TOP TIP

If you add a second heart in contrasting paper and glue only the edges together, you can make a little heart-shaped bag!

1. Using a lead pencil and the templates at the back of the book (page 183), trace and cut out a large heart. Using the next-size-down heart template, cut out a heart from the inside, so you have a heart frame.

2. Use a glue stick to add glue to the outside of the heart frame. Glue on your paper strips in a crisscross fashion. Next, trim the edges.

3. Glue the heart onto contrasting paper and trim to the outside of the frame.

4. Finally, make 2 holes at the top with a hole punch and hang.

# SPRING & EASTER

As the seasons turn and we head into spring and Easter, it is time to refresh our decor and brighten things up. We love all the cute motifs that the season brings, from adorable chicks to flowers!

Whether you are decorating your home or the Easter table, here are some great paper crafts to get you started. This chapter introduces some wonderful basic origami and paper-folding techniques, which will help develop your paper-folding skills. We will work on some origami, so-called witch's ladders and accordion folding.

## CRAFTS IN THIS CHAPTER

# 3-D BUNNY
# PAPER CHAINS

These super-duper cute paper chains can be cut from scrap paper or simply printer paper, making this a great frugal Easter decoration for you! Make them small or make them big— either way, they are just too cute not to have a go at.

## MATERIALS
- White paper

## TOOLS
- Lead pencil
- Scissors
- Pens (optional)
- Glue stick (optional, for larger paper chains)

## TOP TIP
We find cutting up to 4 bunnies per strip manageable. If you start cutting more, the paper gets very stiff and it is much harder to cut. Alternatively, make your bunnies bigger or use thinner newspaper as your paper, to cut out more in one go!

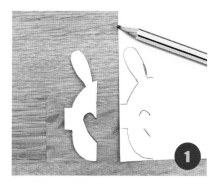
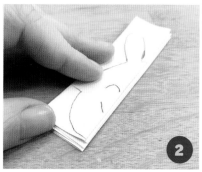

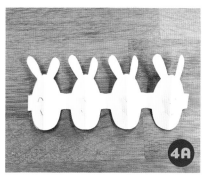

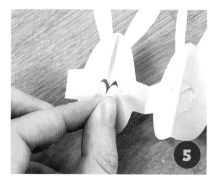

1. Using a lead pencil, trace the bunny template at the back of this book (page 181). Or design your own! Make sure that any design is symmetrical and that you can fold your design in half, then cut out. Copy the design to the edge of your paper strip.

2. Fold along the central line of each bunny and accordion-fold your paper. Make your folds as neatly as possible—the neater and more aligned they are, the cuter your final bunny paper chain will be.

3. Cut out your bunny outline. Note that you must not cut through *all* of the heart, as you want it to stay connected. If you do cut out the heart fully, you will still have an adorable paper chain, but just with a heart-shaped hole in the middle!

4. Unfold and add any details in pen that you wish to add, such as coloring the heart in a desired color and adding bunny facial features.

5. Reverse the heart fold by squeezing it into the opposite direction. This will make your bunny heart pop out.

6. Repeat as many times as you wish and glue your individual bunny chains together.

# 3-D PAPER
## ACCORDION FLOWERS

Once you have made one of these paper flowers, you will find that you want to make more and more. Experimenting with different sized papers, colors and petal shapes. You can use these in spring, summer or winter, depending on what you choose. Reds make beautiful poinsettias; pastels are great for spring!

## MATERIALS

- ½ printer paper, in main color
- ¼ printer paper, in secondary color
- Paper scraps, for decorating (optional)

## TOOLS

- Lead pencil (optional)
- Scissors
- Stapler
- Glue stick or PVA glue (optional)

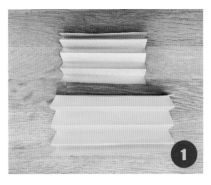

**1.** Fold each piece of paper across its width into exactly 8 sections. The easiest way to get this done neatly is to keep folding the paper in half, then unfolding it and refolding your paper in accordion style along the creases made. You can make the petals pop out or pop in.

**2.** For the leaf to pop *out* at you, take your accordion-folded paper, point the open flap toward your scissors and cut a curve. You may want to draw this with a lead pencil first. You can make the petal pointy or round, depending on your desired final look.

**3.** For the paper flower petal to pop *away* from you, you need to have the closed flap of the accordion-folded paper facing your scissors and cut a similar curve, this time with the top of your curve ending on the open flap.

**4.** Now, fold both accordion-folded papers in the middle: Make a crease halfway and fold it in both directions, so the crease easily works both ways.

**5.** Unfold both sheets and lay over each other. Slot the accordion folds together, with their middle folds lining up.

**6.** Find the center fold and staple as close to the center as possible. Making sure the stapler staples both the sheets of paper together.

(continued)

# 3-D PAPER ACCORDION FLOWERS (CONT.)

**7.** Now comes the *magic* part. Take the top and bottom of 1 side of the accordion and fold it toward each other—one half of the flower is finished. Secure with a staple. Repeat on the other side. When stapling, try to "catch" the contrasting color of your flower, too, to secure it in place.

**8.** You can now glue on decorative details, such as little dots or additional leaves.

# EGG
# CUPS

Spring crafting wouldn't be the same without some simple egg cups! These are easy to make and can be easily adapted to fit any egg size—(whether you like to eat large eggs or small, these will fit any egg you wish). They would look great with decorated "bunny eggs" and "chick eggs" popped inside.

## MATERIALS
- Green paper, about 6 x 4¾" (15.3 x 12 cm)
- Paper scraps, for embellishing

## TOOLS
- Ruler
- Scissors
- Pens
- Glue stick
- Tape or stapler

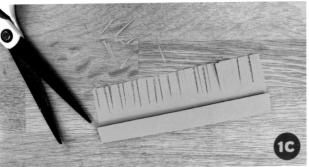

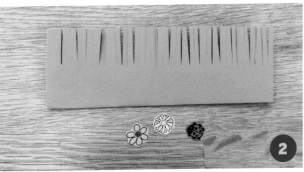

1. Fold your paper 3 times along the 6-inch (15.3-cm) edge. This will make the egg cup nice and strong. Snip into the top of the remaining green paper to make ¾- to 1¼-inch (2- to 3-cm) strips. You can further trim them into narrow triangles if you wish.

2. Draw some embellishments in contrasting colors, using scrap paper—e.g., small flowers, bees and ladybirds—then, cut out and stick around the uncut portion of the folded green paper.

3. Curve your "grass" around and fit 1 end of the base inside the other end. It will most probably hold by itself, but a little tape or a staple will help secure it quickly! Bend the grass blades outward a little and pop in your eggs!

# EASTER
# BASKETS

These super fun baskets are made from one sheet of light card. Although we have decorated them as Easter baskets here, why not draw inspiration from the rest of the book and see how else you could decorate them? Maybe with a flower for Mother's Day or a ghoulish Frankenstein's monster for Halloween? (See the Fall & Halloween chapter [page 147] for Frankenstein's monster design ideas.) This is one great paper basket pattern that you can use all year around!

## MATERIALS

- Light card stock is ideal, though paper will work, too
- Scraps of paper, for decorating

## TOOLS

- Ruler
- Lead pencil
- Scissors
- Stapler
- Pen
- Glue stick

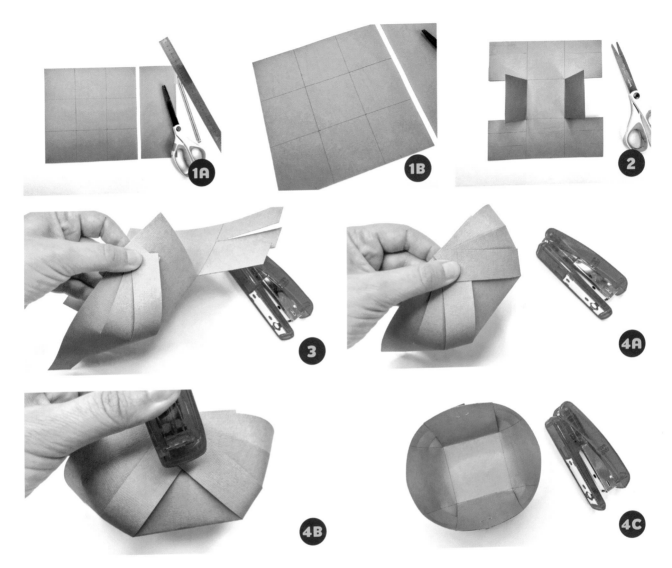

1. This is a craft that benefits from accuracy, so try to work as neatly as you can. Measure out the side of card stock and use a lead pencil to draw a square the same width. Then, draw 2 lines across the square to divide it into 3 equal parts. In this case, a little less than 2¾ inches (7 cm) each. Cut off the edge of the card stock but save this, you will need it for the handle.

2. Using the lines to guide you, make 2 cuts into either side of the square. Fold these up.

3. The first quadrant also needs to have an additional 2 cuts made to create 3 strips. Take these 3 strips and align the top 1 with the side panel, then arrange the others below. Hold tight.

4. Repeat on the other side, until all 3 strips meet in the center panel, and staple in place. Use 2 staples, if needed. Repeat for the other side. Your basic basket shape is finished.

(continued)

# EASTER BASKETS (CONT.)

**5.** Cut a 1¼-inch (3 cm)-wide strip from the remaining card stock and staple it into place to make a basket handle. You can decorate it first, if you wish. Your basket is now finished and just needs decorating!

## TO DECORATE

**6.** Use the basic shapes in the image to guide you to create your own Easter-themed decorations. Stick with simple shapes—ovals, circles, triangles—to create adorable chicks and bunnies! Use a glue stick to glue the shapes together and add to your basket!

How would you turn these into Christmas or Thanksgiving baskets? What could you add?

# 3-D PAPER
## HEN & CHICKS

Learn how to make this basic origami cup shape and turn it into a mother hen with its chicks for Easter. These little chicks could easily hide some chocolate mini Easter eggs or they could make great Easter decoration. Once you have learned how to make these paper cups, what else can you turn them into?

## MATERIALS
- White printer paper
- Yellow printer paper
- Paper scraps, for details

## TOOLS
- Ruler
- Scissors
- Pens
- Glue stick

1. One sheet of white paper can make 2 mother hens: cut into 5½-inch (14-cm) squares. One sheet of yellow paper can be cut down to make 4 paper chicks, each about 4¼-inches (10.8-cm) square.

2. Fold 1 corner across the diagonal to meet the opposite corner and form a neat crease. This gives you a triangle.

3. Turn the triangle, so you have the long side at the bottom and the large right angle at the top. Pick up the bottom right corner and bring it across to the side on the left. You need to create a parallel line with the bottom.

4. Repeat with the bottom left corner.

5. Fold down the triangular flap.

6. Turn over and repeat on the other side.

7. Now, lift the triangular flap and fold to the *inside* of your paper cup. The cup is now ready to be decorated.

## TO DECORATE

8. Add a red comb, black eyes and wings with pens. Cut out a small triangle for the beak. Open the paper cup and squash down the top of the cup to give the hen's head a comb shape. Glue on the beak. Repeat for the chicks.

What other animals could you make like this? An owl? A cat?

# ORIGAMI
## TULIPS

Origami is a wonderful paper-folding technique that is great to learn and get the hang of. At first, many find origami a little tricky to get lines straight and creases tight, so it is good to start with a simple yet pretty project. This origami project is perfect for beginners, providing a great introduction to this classic paper-crafting activity. We love the paper tulips as a "bunch of flowers" in a vase, but they would also look great as part of a collage or greeting card!

## MATERIALS
- 1 square piece of paper, 4" (10-cm) square
- Green paper, 11 x 3⅛" (27.8 x 8 cm)

## TOOLS
- Ruler
- Toothpick or thin paintbrush, to shape the stem
- Glue stick
- Scissors

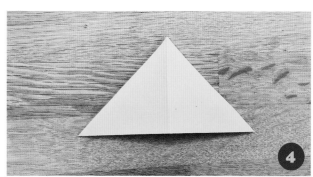

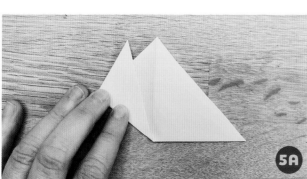

1. Turn the square piece of paper so you have a diamond in front of you.

2. Fold up the bottom point to meet the top point and make a nice, neat crease running along the center. You now should have triangle in front you.

3. Take the right point and bring it all the way over to the left point, making a new smaller triangle.

4. Open it up again. You again should have the triangle from the second step, but now with a crease down the middle, which will help shape your tulip.

5. Flip your paper over and bring the bottom left corner up. This time, you are *not* aligning it with the top point, but are bringing it to about ⅜ inch (1 cm) away from the top point. Repeat with the right side.

(continued)

# ORIGAMI TULIPS (CONT.)

**6.** Your basic paper tulip is finished, but we shall shape it a little more. Flip the tulip over. With all 3 points of the flower at the top, fold in the sides to shape your flower.

**7.** The basic tulip is now finished and can be used for greeting cards, collages or bouquets of flowers.

## MAKE THE STEM

**8.** Take the green paper strip and start rolling it up diagonally; using a toothpick or a thin paintbrush to get it going should help. Using a glue stick, secure with a little glue.

**9.** Make a little snip into the bottom of your tulip flower and insert the stem. You may want to glue the stem in place.

# SIMPLE
# PAPER SHEEP

Another super quick and easy paper craft for Easter and spring. These sheep use
a fun paper-folding technique—you will want to make hundreds of these once you start.
What other animals can you come up with?

## MATERIALS

- White printer paper
- Scraps of black and pink paper, for the face
- Paper clips*

*Instead of paper clips, you can glue pipe cleaners in place or make little legs from light card stock or recycled cereal boxes.

## TOOLS

- Ruler
- Scissors
- Glue stick
- Pen

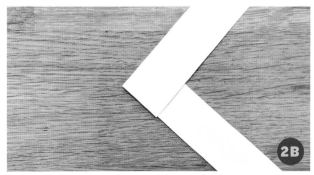

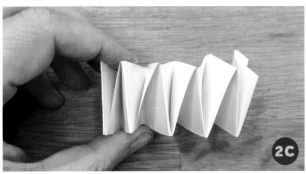

1. To begin, cut 2 long strips of paper, each 11 x 1¼ inches (27.9 x 3 cm).

2. Glue 2 ends together at *right* angles. Now, fold the lower strip of paper over the top of the second strip. Repeat by folding the second strip over the first, and so on. Continue until you have no more paper left, then use a glue stick to secure with glue.

3. To make the sheep's face, we will use simple shapes again—an oval for the head, teardrops with the ends flattened for the ears and a little cloud shape for the top of the head. Glue all your pieces together. Add any details in black pen, or glue on pink rosy cheeks and little paper eyes. Then, glue the head to the top of your accordion-folded sheep.

4. Finally, add paper clips for legs!

# SUMMER FUN

Aaaah, those long summer months! Time to keep yourself busy! Although, of course, you can make anything from this book during the summer, here are some great summer-specific crafts to make.

Once again, we have crafts for decorating with or to add to notebooks or greeting cards, but also crafts that you can play with. See how easy it is to make some paper helicopters or fun paper kites (they are so quick to make, you will be surprised!), or put on a show with the Paper Dog Puppets (page 136).

For decorating there are Paper Fish (page 140) and 3-D Paper Cactus (page 130) plants. Why not make the Llama Cards, page 70, to go with them, too? Lots of ideas to keep you going.

In this chapter, we hone our paper-folding skills when making Accordion Bugs (page 142), and marvel at the magic of symmetry and paper cutting when making Kirigami Butterflies (page 138) and a Strawberry Box (page 126)!

## CRAFTS IN THIS CHAPTER

# STRAWBERRY BOX

A pretty little paper decoration for summer. These 3-D strawberries can be used as decor (string them up on some ribbon) or used to hold a little treat. Fill with a chocolate and give to a friend!

## MATERIALS

- Red paper
- Medium green paper scraps
- Ribbon or thread, for closing
- Small treat or gift (optional)

## TOOLS

- Lead pencil
- Small salad plate, for measuring (a 6" [15-cm] diameter is good)
- Tin can, for measuring (a 3" [7.5-cm] diameter is good)
- Scissors
- Hole punch
- Pen
- Glue stick or PVA glue (optional)

1. Using a lead pencil, trace around your plate on the red paper and around the tin can on the green paper, and cut out both of your circles. Beginning with your red circle, fold it in half.

2. Then, fold it in half again 2 more times. Use the pencil to draw a petal shape on your folded circle. The petal should go from the middle of the first edge to the top of the curve, then back down to the middle of the second edge. Cut this out and hole punch the top of the petal. Open it up and you should have a flower shape. Cut one-quarter out as you won't need this.

(continued)

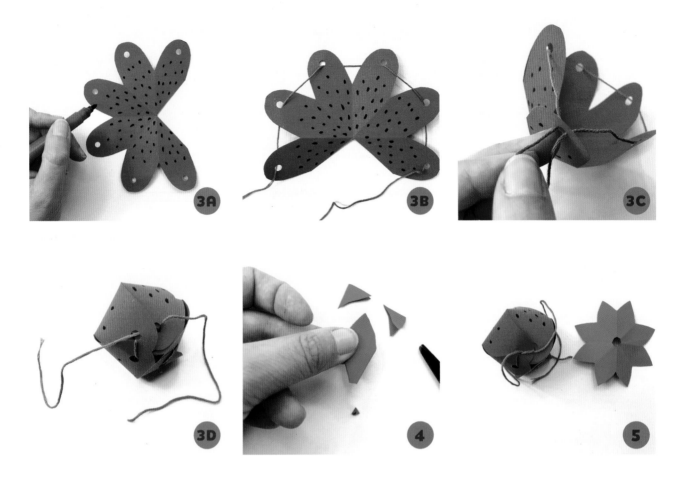

# STRAWBERRY BOX (CONT.)

3. Use a pen to add some black dots as strawberry seeds. Next, thread a ribbon or thread through the holes, threading the end that has exited last back through the first hole and pulling, so the strawberry will come together and form into a 3-D shape. Now, secure by tying a bow or knot (fill the strawberry first if you want to use it as a gift box).

4. To make the strawberry's leaf, repeat the folding steps from the beginning, using the green circle. This time, however, make your petal shape pointy at the top (for a leaf) and snip away a small part at the bottom—this will give you a hole for threading.

5. Open it up. Pop the tied thread through the center of your strawberry leaf and you're done. You may wish to add a little glue to the bottom of the leaf to secure it, but it isn't strictly necessary.

# 3-D PAPER CACTUS

These paper cacti are super quick and easy to make. What is particularly fabulous about them is that you don't need a template, so you can create all sorts of wonderful and interesting shapes, making each cactus unique. Make them large or small—depending on your decorating needs!

## MATERIALS

- Per medium-size cactus:
  3 half sheets of green printer paper
- Paper scraps, for decorating

## TOOLS

- Glue stick
- Lead pencil
- Scissors
- Pens

### TOP TIP

Scrunched-up tissue paper would make lovely little cactus flowers, too!

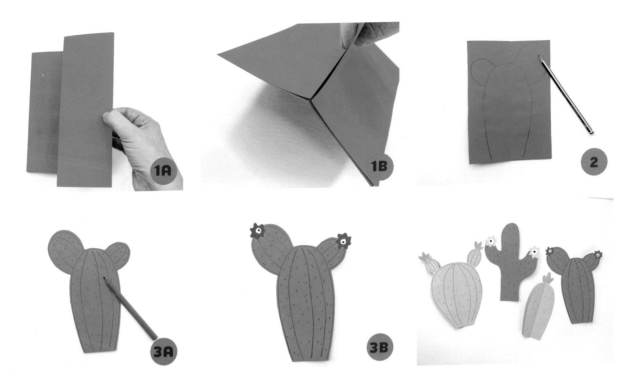

1. Fold each sheet of paper in half lengthwise. Using a glue stick, add glue to 1 side of 1 sheet of paper. Place a second sheet of paper on top of the first sheet and glue them together, making sure the creases are on the same side. Repeat with the second and third sheets of paper, until all 3 sheets are glued together into a stack. Add glue to the outside of the top sheet of paper, fold open and glue to the side on the bottom sheet.

2. Flatten again and use a lead pencil to draw the outline of a cactus. Above are 4 examples for you to be inspired by. Then, cut out the cactus shape.

3. Add some decorations with pens. If you wish, you can also cut out simple flowers from differently colored scrap paper and glue them on! Repeat the decorations on all sides. Open up and your first cactus is finished!

# KITE
# BIRDS

A super quick and easy kite to make on a windy afternoon. Decorate in bright colors and have fun outdoors. If the kite gets damaged, don't worry—make another one!

## MATERIALS
- 1 sheet of white printer paper
- String (the thinner but stronger, the better)

## TOOLS
- Pens
- Ruler
- Stapler
- Hole punch

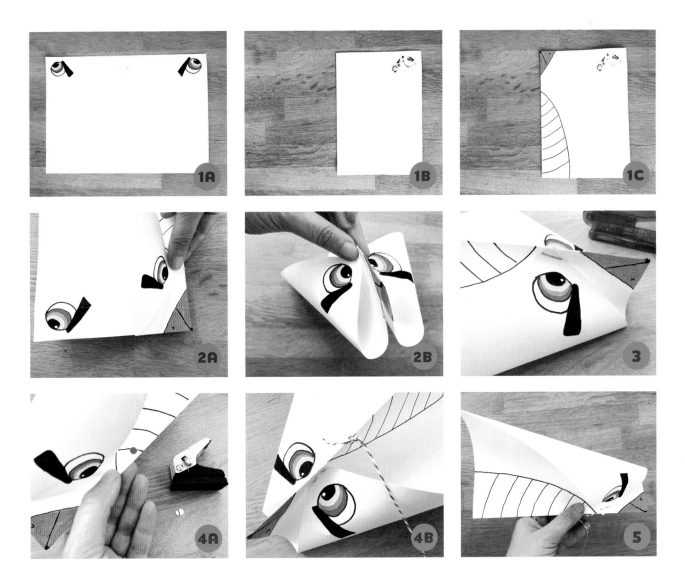

1. You can make a plain kite or decorate it like a bird first! If decorating, begin by drawing 2 large eyes in the top left and right corners of the paper. See the photo steps for the positioning of the eyes. Fold the paper in half widthwise, keeping the eyes on the *inside* of the paper. Then, decorate with a beak and a tummy.

2. Hold the beak toward you. Bring the corner of the paper with an eye up toward you and position it about 2 inches (5 cm) from the paper's edge, or just below the beak. Repeat on the other side.

3. Secure with a stapler. Your basic kite is made!

4. Using a hole punch, make a hole ⅜ to ¾ inch (1 to 2 cm) below the staple and tie on some string (about 5 feet [1.5 m] is a good length).

Go fly your kite!

# HELICOPTER
# FUN

A great project for using up scraps of paper and learning a little science. You can make these paper helicopters quickly and easily and then while away the afternoon playing with them.

## MATERIALS

- Strips of paper, about 8½ x 1¼"
  (21.8 x 3 cm)
- Scraps of paper, for decorating
  (optional)
- Paper clips

## TOOLS

- Ruler
- Scissors
- Glue stick (optional)

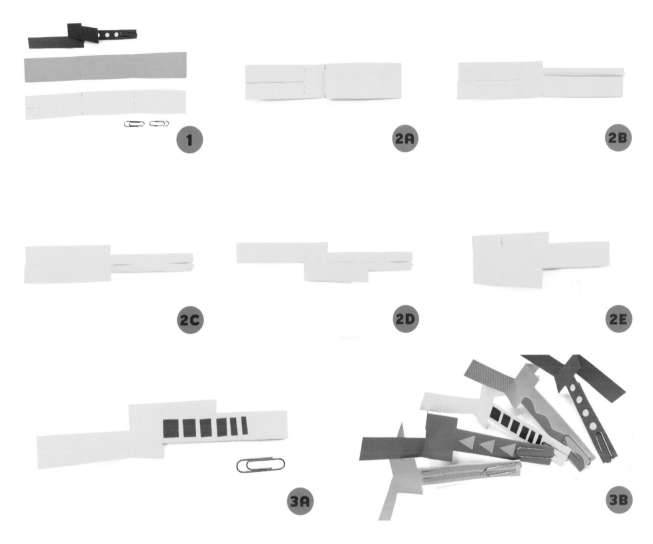

1. Fold each strip of paper roughly into 3 parts. Bring the bottom third of the paper up and make a neat crease.

2. Cut ¼-inch (5-mm) snips on both sides of the top fold. Fold the double sheets of paper inward along these snips, making a thicker base. Cut about ¼ inch (5 mm) down the center of the remaining top third of the original paper strip. Fold down the created flaps in opposite directions to make the helicopter blades.

3. Decorate with contrasting colored paper scraps, if you wish, and add a paper clip, for additional weight, to each helicopter.

4. Experiment with what happens with no paper clip, 1 paper clip and 2 paper clips: Does your helicopter spin better or faster?

# PAPER
# DOG PUPPET

A super fun and simple paper hand puppet! We are decorating ours as a cute little dog; however, you can turn these puppets into anything you'd like.

## MATERIALS

- 1 sheet of printer paper
- Paper scraps, for decorating

## TOOLS

- Glue stick or tape
- Scissors
- Pen

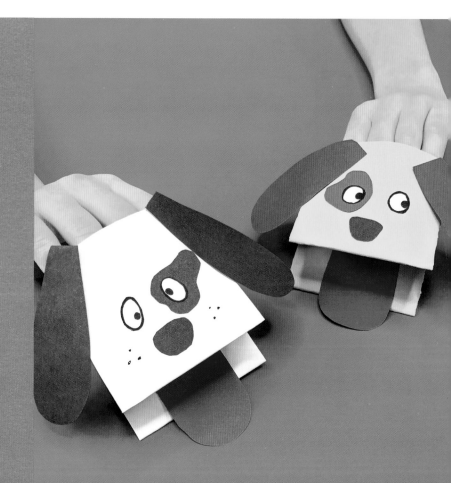

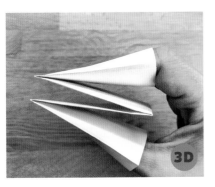

1. Take the long edge of your sheet of paper and fold it in one-third of the way. Take the other long edge and also fold it in one-third of the way. You should have 1 long sheet of paper folded twice and a third of its original width (roughly 3 inches [7.5 cm] wide).

2. Glue or tape down the top piece of paper.

3. Flip over and fold in half widthwise. Fold 1 of the flaps up. Turn over and fold the other flap up. You should now have a *W*-shaped fold. Your fingers will be able to slot into the top and bottom parts.

4. Time to decorate! For a dog, you will need 2 ears, a tongue, nose and eyes. Add an eye patch if you wish! Use a glue stick to glue on all the dog's features and add any finishing touches in pen.

What other animals can you design? A cat? A pig? A cow? What features would you need to add for these animals?

# KIRIGAMI
# BUTTERFLIES

Kirigami is the art of paper cutting! You will most probably have made some paper-cut snowflakes before. But there are so many other things you can create using this technique! Make these butterflies to decorate your room, notebooks, greeting cards and more! Have a go at experimenting with different shapes and patterns.

## MATERIALS

- 2 squares of colored paper, about 4¾" (12-cm) square

## TOOLS

- Lead pencil
- Scissors
- Glue stick

## TOP TIP

Practice with scrap paper first and experiment with different shapes and patterns!

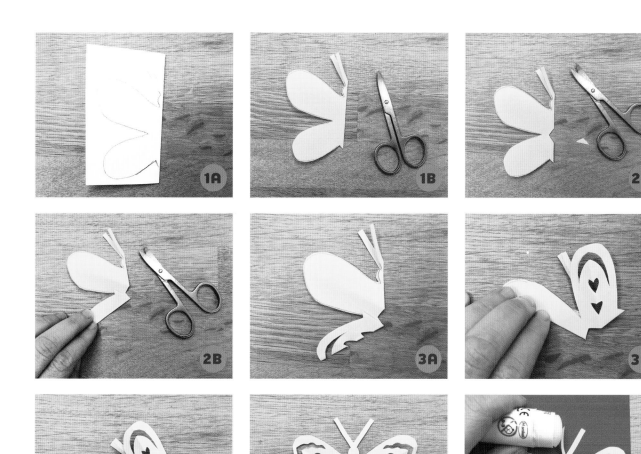

1. Fold your paper in half and use a lead pencil to draw or trace half of a butterfly outline (page 182) onto it, positioning it vertically along the fold. Cut out and keep the paper folded.

2. Cut a shape into the center of your butterfly (where the main body is)—try half a heart, a circle or a triangle. You can cut more than 1 shape if you wish. Keeping the paper folded, fold the bottom wing in half lengthwise.

3. Cut some patterns into the folded bottom wing. Repeat with the top wing.

4. Carefully unfold. Your basic butterfly is finished! You can stick it onto tissue paper as a sun catcher, colored paper to decorate walls or straight onto a notebook or colorful card.

Experiment with other bugs and shapes, such as a dragonfly.

# PAPER FISH

Quirky little fish made from scraps of paper! Have fun with colors and decorate with pens.
These paper fish would look wonderful hanging from a mobile, too.

## MATERIALS

- Strips of paper, about 8½ x 2"
  (21.8 x 5 cm)
- Scraps of contrasting colored
  paper, for decorating

## TOOLS

- Ruler
- Scissors
- Pen
- Glue stick

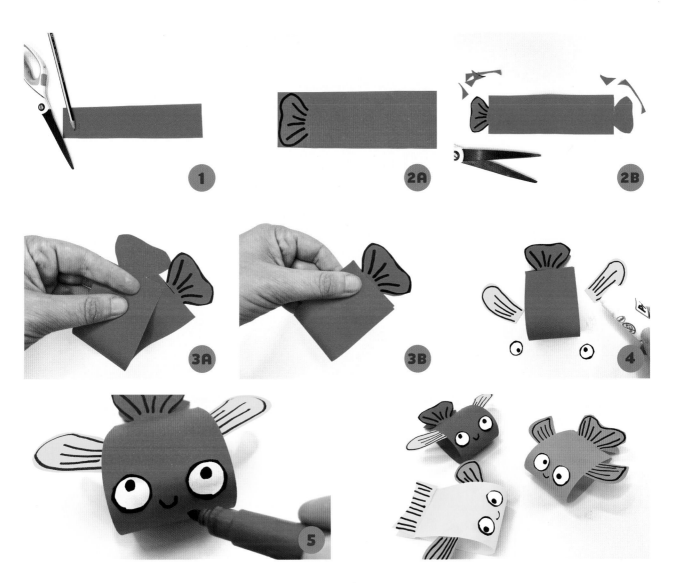

1. About 1 inch (2.5 cm) from the top of a strip of paper, cut a slit that goes halfway across, from right to left. Repeat at the bottom of the strip of paper, but this time, cut a slit from *left* to *right*, so the slits are on opposite sides.

2. Decorate these end pieces as fins. Trim if you wish.

3. Fold your piece of paper over and slot the 2 slits together! If they don't fit together neatly, just snip a little extra into your slit until they fit properly!

4. Cut 2 paper fins and 2 eyes from your scrap paper. Add details in black ink.

5. Use a glue stick to glue on the fins and eyes. You can have fun with the positioning of the eyes! Add a little mouth, using a pen.

# ACCORDION BUGS

What would summer be without some bugs! As you may have guessed, I love the accordion paper-folding technique; it is so effective and so easy to do. Turn your accordions into paper bugs today. How can you decorate their backs and make them all different? What color would you make yours?

## MATERIALS
- 1 piece of paper at least 6" (15-cm) square
- Contrasting paper, for decorating

## TOOLS
- Lead pencil
- Salad plate, about 6" (15 cm) in diameter, for tracing
- Scissors
- Ruler
- Pen
- Glue stick

1. Use a lead pencil to trace around the plate to create a circle on the paper. Cut it out. Fold the circle in half and cut in half. Each half will make 1 accordion bug. Beginning at the long straight edge, fold up the paper by about ¼ inch (5 mm). Keep folding, accordion style, until you get to the end.

2. If you want to add stripes to your bug, open the accordion and color every other section black. Be careful not to smudge it. Refold!

(continued)

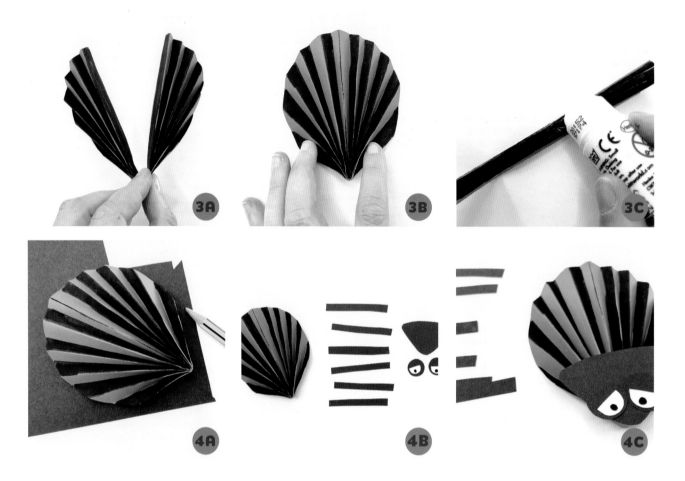

# ACCORDION BUGS (CONT.)

**3.** Take your folded accordion and fold it in half, so that the long edges meet in the middle. Use a glue stick to add a little glue and glue the *long* edges together.

**4.** Trace the curved edged to make a triangular head for your bug. Cut additional features, such as black circles with white semicircles for eyes and black legs. Glue the face together and add it to your bug. Glue the legs onto the back of the paper bug; you may have to fold them into the accordion to secure.

# FALL & HALLOWEEN

Fall is a great time to head back indoors and get crafty. With all those wonderful fall colors for inspiration and the spooky Halloween season ahead, this a fun time to start creating.

In this chapter, you will learn a clever trick to turn paper into a little treat box (page 160) quickly and easily, see how easy it is to make paper Ghost Garlands (page 162) (providing inspiration for all the other seasons, too) and have fun with witch's ladders and accordion folding. So many great ideas. Again, we break designs down into simple shapes that allow you to turn circles and triangles into turkeys or owls!

## CRAFTS IN THIS CHAPTER

# LEAF WREATH

This great wreath can be used throughout fall and for Thanksgiving. Making the leaves is quick and easy and you can turn them not only into a wreath or garland, but add them to some twigs and create a thankfulness tree. So, depending on the needs of your decor, you have a choice of how to use your paper leaves!

## MATERIALS

- Paper in fall colors
- 1 dinner plate–size paper plate, or a large cereal box
- Ribbon, for hanging

## TOOLS

- Pen
- Scissors
- Stapler or tape
- Glue stick

1. Either draw your own leaf template or use the one in the back of the book (page 181). You can also find real leaves and trace them (though they tend to be a lot bigger!). Trace your leaf shapes onto colorful paper and cut them out. The cutting doesn't have to be super neat; it can be effective to leave the pen mark showing! You can layer your paper and cut out several at a time, if you wish to!

2. Add any additional details using a black pen. If you cut several leaves in one go, also add a black outline. Make 18 to 22 leaves. If you give the leaves a little fold, you can make them pop out from your wreath at bit more!

3. Cut a hole into the center of your paper plate to create a tire shape. If using a cereal box, use a dinner plate and a salad plate to trace and cut it. Staple or tape some ribbon to the back of it, for hanging.

4. Glue on your paper leaves, using a glue stick. Try to spread out the different shapes and colors!

Pick a spot to hang your lovely paper wreath!

# OWL
## PAPER FAN

These paper fan owls are bright and cheerful! Choose the color of the body of your owl based on what colored paper you have the most of (they can even be white owls, using printer paper). These owls make great party decorations or cute Halloween decorations. What a hoot! They got a huge thumbs-up from both my kids! As with all the crafts in this book, once you have learned the basics of how to make a paper fan, what else can you turn this into? Wouldn't a snowman with an orange nose and charcoal eyes look fabulous? Or maybe turn it into a jack-o'-lantern for Halloween?

## MATERIALS
- 1½ sheets of printer paper, in your main color (e.g., yellow)
- Contrasting colored scrap paper
- White paper
- Thread or baker's twine, for hanging (optional)

## TOOLS
- Scissors
- Ruler
- Glue stick
- Pens

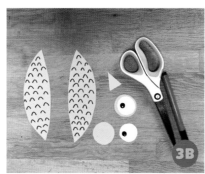

1. Cut the whole sheet of main colored paper in half—you will need 3 halves, each 5½ x 8½ inches (14 x 21.6 cm). Or you can use full-size sheets, if you wish to make larger decorations. Accordion-fold all 3 half-sheets of paper along the *long* edge, making the folds ¼ inch (5 mm) apart. If using 3 full sheets, make the folds ⅜ inch (1 cm) apart. Then fold each folded sheet up the middle.

2. Begin by gluing the 2 inner edges of each sheet of paper together, using a glue stick. Then, glue the sides of each adjacent fold to the next, until the folds are fanned into a circle. The last 2 sides to come together will be a little fiddly and you will have to hold them together a bit longer!

3. Now it is time to create the features. Use the owl's main body to roughly trace out the shape of a wing. Cut 2 wings, 2 large eyes, 2 smaller eyes and a triangular beak from your scrap paper. Add features in pen. Add lots of glue to the back of your features and glue them onto your accordion-folded disks! If you wish to hang your owl, use a little glue to secure some baker's twine to the back of it!

# 3-D
# PUMPKIN

I love making 3-D decorations from paper. I will show you one paper technique here that is suitable for ornaments and encourage you to think about how you can change it for other seasons. Maybe you can adapt the polar bear features from the Christmas chapter (page 170)? Here is a fabulous 3-D pumpkin that you can use throughout fall—maybe add a little jack-o'-lantern face to it for Halloween? Your pumpkin can stand on a shelf or can be hung on a ribbon or as part of a fall mobile or garland. Add thankful messages to each section and your pumpkin will work wonderfully as a Thanksgiving activity, too!

## MATERIALS
- Orange paper
- Green paper scraps
- Black paper scraps (optional)

## TOOLS
- A glass or tin can, for tracing
- Lead pencil
- Scissors
- Glue stick

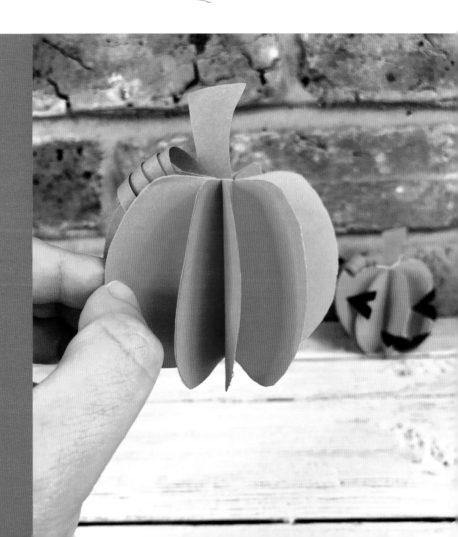

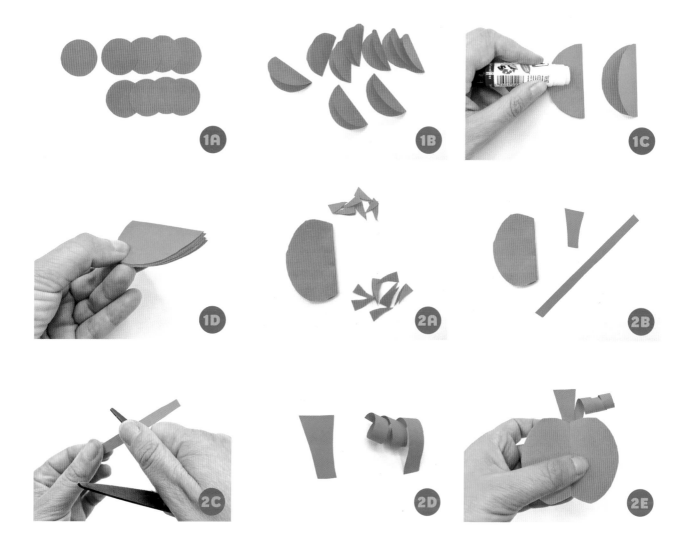

1. Using a glass or tin can and a lead pencil, trace 8 to 10 circles onto the orange paper and cut them out. Fold your circles in half. Use a glue stick to add glue to half of a circle and then place a second circle on top, so that 2 semicircles are glued together, with the other half of each free. Repeat until all your circles stacked.

2. Trim the top and bottom of your circles to give them a pumpkin shape. Cut a short green stem, plus a long strip of green paper. Using scissors, carefully curl the paper strip to become a vine. Ask an adult for help if you need to. Add a little glue to the stem and the vine, and nudge them in between the layers at 1 edge of the orange circle.

(continued)

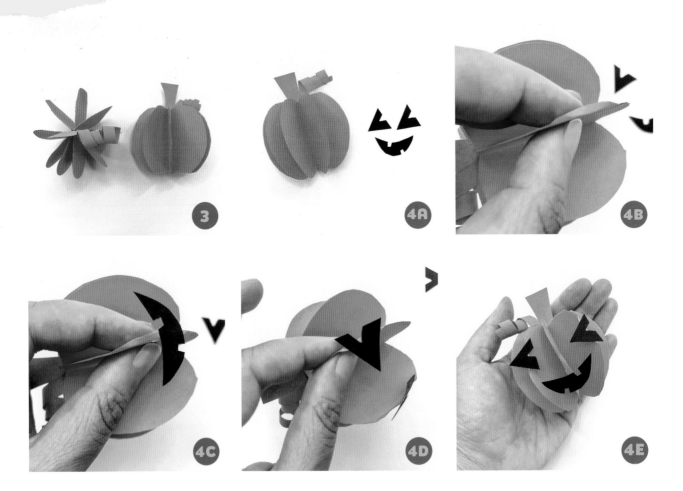

# 3-D PUMPKIN (CONT.)

**3.** Add glue to the outside semicircles and press them together to form your 3-D shape. Your basic pumpkin is finished.

**4.** Want to turn it into a jack-o'-lantern? Cut some jack-o'-lantern shapes from black paper. Turn the central paper fold of the pumpkin into a tiny flap—only $\frac{1}{32}$ to $\frac{1}{16}$ inch (1 to 1.5 mm) wide. Then, glue the mouth to it. Repeat with the paper folds on either side to add the eyes.

# TURKEY NAPKIN RINGS

Super-duper fun and cute napkin rings for fall and Thanksgiving. These napkin rings are indeed made from paper, but can also be made from felt (use a hot glue gun or some simple stitches) or can be strengthened by adding card stock or cardboard. You can have lots of fun adapting these—adding thankful messages to the turkey's tail feathers or adding place names to either feathers or a small white rectangle across the turkey's body!

## MATERIALS
- Brown paper or card stock
- A paper towel tube or cardboard from a cereal box (optional)
- Paper scraps in white, yellow, orange and red

## TOOLS
- Ruler
- Scissors
- Glue stick
- Lead pencil
- Pens

1. Cut a strip of brown paper, 2 x 6 inches (5 x 15 cm), or long enough to wrap around your paper towel tube if you wish to line it with one. Use a glue stick to glue the short edges together to make a little brown tube. This will be the main napkin ring holder. You can strengthen your napkin ring, if you wish by using brown card stock instead, gluing 2 strips of brown paper together, or gluing the single-ply strip to a paper towel tube or a piece of cereal box cardboard cut to the same size as the strip.

2. Using a lead pencil, mark and cut your turkey's paper parts: 1 large circle about 2 inches (5 cm) wide (i.e., about the diameter of your paper tube) and a smaller circle (maybe half the size). These are only approximations and each turkey will have its own character and personality depending on what you cut. Also cut a beak, a wattle and some eyes. Add the pupils with a pen, though, of course, you can use googly eyes instead.

3. Assemble your turkey's body by gluing it together with a glue stick. You can really give each turkey a different character depending on what size you make the eyes and where you place them!

4. Cut 5 (or more!) turkey feathers from colored paper scraps. Choose colors to go with your Thanksgiving decor or use the traditional: yellow, orange and red! You can also decorate these with pens, if you wish, or add thankful messages. Glue their base along the back of your turkey's body. Then glue the turkey to your paper napkin ring.

# ACCORDION
# SPIDER

Accordion-folding paper is easy and super fun. The effect is cool and can be used on so many projects! I asked my kids what accordion-folded craft they thought should go in this book and my son immediately suggested a spider. What a great choice, as those spidery legs are perfect for a paper accordion!

## MATERIALS
- 1 sheet each of black and purple paper
- Thread or baker's twine, for hanging
- White paper scraps

## TOOLS
- Paper cutter (optional)
- Scissors
- Ruler
- Glue stick
- Small plate (optional)
- Pens

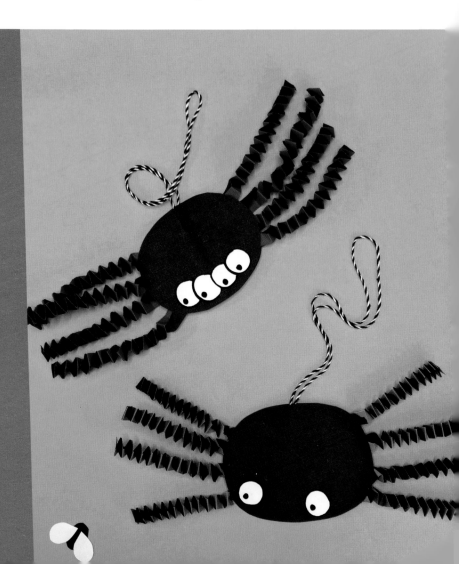

**1.** Begin by making a "witch's ladder": Cut 8 (⅜-inch [1-cm]-wide) strips of black paper and 8 strips of purple paper. I used the long side of an 8½ x 11-inch (21.6 x 27.9–cm) sheet of paper; if your paper dimensions are a little different, that is fine; just make them as long as possible. If you have a paper cutter, use that; otherwise, take your time and cut your paper carefully!

**2.** Glue the end of a strip black paper onto the end of a strip of purple paper at a right angle.

**3.** Now, fold the lower strip of paper over the top of the second strip. Repeat, alternating colors, by folding the second strip over the first and so on. Continue until you have no more paper left along the strips and then secure the ends with glue. Repeat to form a total of 8 accordion-folded 2-tone legs.

**4.** Cut 2 ovals or circles for the spider's body—we used the remaining black paper. The size is a question of preference. You can trace around a small plate, if it helps. Use a glue stick to glue the end of 4 legs to 1 side of an oval and the ends of the other 4 legs to its opposite side.

**5.** Cut some thread or baker's twine for hanging. Add glue to the back of oval to which the legs are attached, place the second disk on top and make sure you insert the end of hanging thread to the top, too! Press the 2 disks together to secure.

**6.** Finally, draw some eyes onto white paper. This is the bit where your paper spider really comes to life and you can experiment with positions and number of eyes. Each position/type of eye will give your spider a different character. I was going to use 2 eyes, but my daughter said 5 looked more fun . . .

# PYRAMID
# HALLOWEEN
# TREAT BOXES

Quick and easy paper treat boxes to make for Halloween! Decorate them in as many different spooky ways that you can think of! We have made these out of paper, but light card stock is great, too.

## MATERIALS

- Paper strips, about 3 x 6" (7.5 x 15 cm), in desired colors (e.g., white, orange, purple and green) (If you prefer a different size, keep to a 2:1 ratio).
- Treats for your treat boxes
- Paper scraps in white or black

## TOOLS

- Scissors
- Glue stick, tape or staples
- Pens

## TOP TIP

Make these treat boxes in Christmas colors and they work wonderfully as an advent calendar!

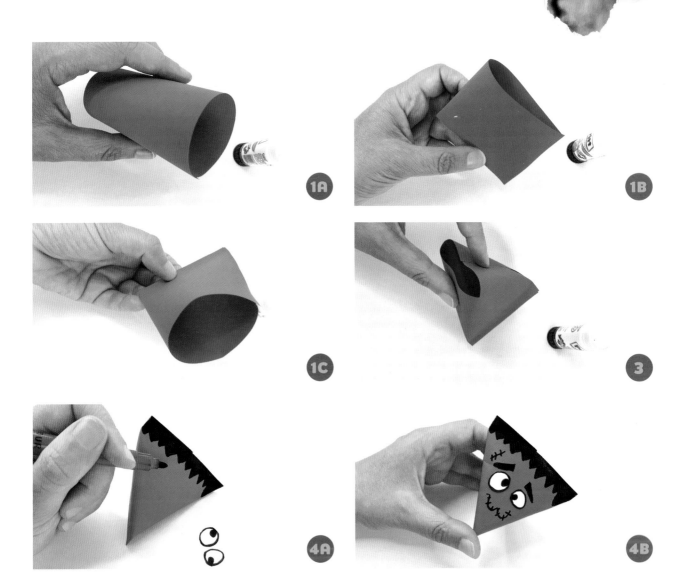

1. Take a strip and using a glue stick, glue the short ends together to make a cylinder. Make a light crease along the edge where you glued your cylinder together. Now, working down along the crease, squeeze 1 open end of the cylinder flat and either glue or tape or staple it down. The other open side is now a loop.

2. Using your thumb and index finger, place your thumb near the crease of the first edge and your index finger opposite. Squeeze your fingers together, forming a new vertical edge. This edge should be perpendicular to the edge you created before!

3. Before you glue this closed, fill with treats! Then, glue, tape or staple shut. You have just made a basic paper pyramid box!

4. Use pens and scraps of paper to decorate— turn your treat boxes into skeletons, ghosts, pumpkins and Frankenstein's monsters!

# QUICK
# GHOST GARLAND

Boo! Do you need a quick and easy decoration for Halloween?! Have a go at these fun little ghost friends. These ghost garlands can be made super long or short—just cut as many ghosts as you wish. A great way to use up scrap pieces of white printer paper. They would also look adorable hanging from a mobile or suspended from some twigs in a vase!

## MATERIALS
- 1 sheet of white printer paper
- String, for hanging

## TOOLS
- Scissors
- Lead pencil
- Hole punch
- Pens

1. Cut the paper in half lengthwise to create 2 long strips, each 4¼ x 5½ inches (10.8 x 27.9 cm). The size need not be exact; work with what you have! Fold in half twice, widthwise. You should now have 4 layers of paper per strip.

2. Use a lead pencil to draw a ghost onto the top layer of the strip of paper. Make it as big as possible, but keep the shape simple to cut out. Cut out your ghost—cutting through 4 sheets in a single go. Repeat for the second strip of paper, making the shape of your ghost a little different this time, if you wish.

3. Using a hole punch, make 2 holes on either side of each ghost around the ghost's arms. Then, add some fun ghost faces with your pens.

4. Finally, it is time to thread the ghosts onto your string—alternating the different shapes.

# CHRISTMAS & WINTER

'Tis the season to get merry. Tra-la-la-laaaa. Last but not least, here is our Christmas crafting session! It's the perfect crafting scenario—long dark afternoons, cozy warm indoors and a nice hot drink to keep you going. Sit down and get crafty. A great time to craft together as a family, decorate your home and get into that festive spirit.

In this chapter, we will have fun with paper strips (see how easy they are turned into an ornament [page 170]), more clever accordion-folding, quick gift bags (page 176) (that you can scale down or up, using brown kraft paper or gift wrap) and quick Christmas tree decorations.

Enjoy and a Merry Christmas to you!

## CRAFTS IN THIS CHAPTER

# GINGERBREAD SANTA

A super fun gingerbread man activity for Christmas. Use gingerbread cutters that you may have at home or else the handy template in this book. These Christmas decorations or greeting cards show the versatility of design: one gingerbread man template, three different ways to decorate! I am sure you can come up with more designs of your own.

## MATERIALS
- Light card stock
- Scrap paper

## TOOLS
- Lead pencil
- Scissors
- Glue stick
- Pens

## TOP TIP
You can use just white card for all of your designs and decorate with pens and more paper scraps to obtain your desired colors!

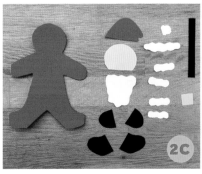
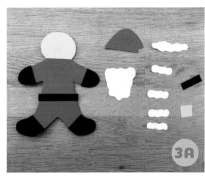

1. Choose the color of your light card according to which Christmas character you would like to make: here we use red for a Santa. Cut out your basic gingerbread man template (page 182). Fold your light card stock in half and align your template against the folded edge and the bottom. The hands and feet have to overlap slightly, so that you get 2 connected figures that can stand up by themself or let you use the folded card stock as a greeting card! Trace around the template, using a lead pencil, then cut through both layers, making sure to leave the figures' hands and feet connected along their common fold.

2. Using your cut card as a size guide and a lead pencil, trace out some Santa boots and gloves. Repeat to trace a face in the desired skin tone and the basic shape/width of Santa's hat and beard. Cut out all your Santa embellishments—2 boots, 2 gloves, white fluffy details, belt and buckle, face, beard and hat.

3. Using a glue stick, start gluing down the features in layers. Glue down your first layer of embellishments—the head, gloves, boots and belt. Glue down the second layer—the beard, hat, white fluffy bits and buckle. Finally add the center of the missing belt buckle and add eyes and a mouth with a pen. This is just one way to decorate Santa. How else could you do yours?

## FOR A SNOWMAN

Use white card stock for the body. Cut a hat with a red ribbon, a carrot nose and "coal" buttons.

## FOR A GINGERBREAD MAN

Use brown card stock for the body. Cut 2 triangles and a circle for the bow tie, some red buttons and a candy cane by drawing red stripes onto white paper at an angle. Then, add some cute pink cheeks.

# PAPER ANGEL

I adore these little paper angels! They are super quick to make and are so cute. This angel is made entirely out of paper—but you can also make the angel's head from wooden beads and add wool or tinsel hair!

## MATERIALS

- 1 square piece of colored or patterned paper, about 6" (15 cm) square
- 1 piece of white paper, about 4 x 6" (10 x 15 cm)
- Paper scraps
- Baker's twine, for hanging
- Gems, bows or sequins (optional)

## TOOLS

- Pens
- Glue stick
- Scissors

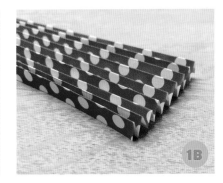

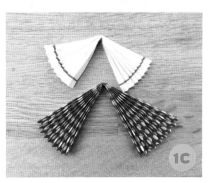

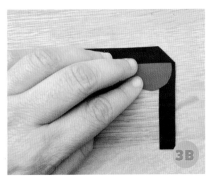

1. Accordion-fold your colored paper square with approximately ¼-inch (5-mm) folds. Take the rectangular white paper. I added some red stripes with a red pen to the white paper for effect, but you can leave the white paper plain, too! Fold the white paper lengthwise into accordion folds.

2. Fold both accordions in half, as neatly as you can. Then, using a glue stick, glue each outermost fold of the white paper wings over the top fold of the body. Tie some baker's twine around the central folds for hanging (and it also secures the shape a little more). Fold the innermost sides of the colored paper together and glue together to form an angel skirt.

3. To make a face, you will need to cut a 1¼-inch (3-cm) circle in a skin-tone color, plus an extra strip of 7 x ⅜-inch (17.8 x 1-cm) paper in your choice of hair color. Glue the strip of paper to the top of the head. Then, fold it down behind the head on both sides. Trim to a desired length. And add your facial features with pens! Finally, glue the head to the top of the angel body and add any desired embellishments, such as gems, bows or sequins.

# POLAR BEAR ORNAMENTS

These adorable Christmas tree decorations are so inexpensive to make—all you need is a little printer paper and you are more or less done. Once you learn how to make this basic paper-strip head, what other designs can you come up with?

## MATERIALS
- Printer paper
- Baker's twine or ribbon, for hanging
- Scraps of blue paper (optional)

## TOOLS
- Ruler
- Scissors
- Glue stick
- Pens

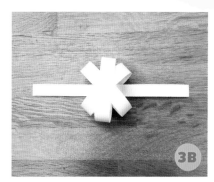

1. If you cut carefully, you can get 8 strips of paper from your 1 sheet of paper, to make 2 polar bears. However, cutting roughly ⅝ x 7⅞-inch (1.5 x 20-cm) strips will make wonderful polar bears, too. You need 4 of these strips per bear. Fold each strip in half lengthwise and gently crease, to mark the center of each strip.

2. Lay one strip over a second strip to make a cross and use a glue stick to glue in place. Repeat with the remaining strips, gluing them in place at diagonals to one another.

3. Bring the 2 ends together and glue, create a circular loop. Add a little glue to the top of the loop and bring up the end of each remaining strip to the center (adding glue as necessary to secure) until there is only 1 unglued end left.

4. Take a little baker's twine or ribbon, knot and place on top your ornament. Glue the remaining strip in place over it to secure it for hanging! Your basic paper-strip ornament is finished.

## TO DECORATE

5. You can choose to add a splash of color or leave your polar bear white. Cut out ears, a mouth and eyes, decorating with a pen where necessary. Make a small fold at the bottom of each ear and glue into place. Finally, glue on the mouth and eyes.

What else could you turn this basic paper ornament into? A snowman's head? A chubby little round bird?

# SIMPLE 3-D
# CHRISTMAS TREES

Remember, when it comes to crafting and decorating, simplicity is often key!
Simple paper crafts can quickly and easily transform your room's decor. These 3-D Christmas
trees are such an example. You will love how easy they are. A great way to
transform a mantelpiece, bookshelf or windowsill in no time!

## MATERIALS
- Green printer paper
- Paper scraps (some in yellow)

## TOOLS
- Ruler
- Lead pencil
- Scissors
- Glue stick
- Hole punch
- Battery-powered tea light (optional)

## TOP TIP
If you want to use tea lights to shine through your tree, make a thinner tree. If you are making confetti Christmas trees, they can be wider.

1. Decide how wide you want the base of your tree to be. Let's say you want your tree to have 3½-inch (9-cm)-wide base. Make a fold in the paper that gives you a 1¾-inch (4.5-cm) flap (i.e. half of the desired tree base). Using a ruler, draw a diagonal from the outer edge of the folded paper to the crease to achieve a tree height of your choosing, such as 5½ inches (14 cm). That is, the line runs from the corner up to a point. Cut along the pencil mark. When you unfold the paper, you should have a 2-sided 5½-inch (14-cm)-tall tree with a base that is 3½ inches (9 cm) wide before folding it to stand up. Play with the tree dimensions and make them any size you wish!

2. Trim a little of the base per the image. This will help your tree stand up and look shapelier—but you can skip this step, if you wish! Using your hole punch, either make neatly spaced-out holes, or punch out colored confetti from the scraps of paper and stick this confetti on with a glue stick.

3. Finally, make a small star by cutting 2 small yellow triangles and gluing them on top of each other. Glue on any additional confetti to finish off your tree. If you have hole-punched your tree, you can pop a little battery-powered tea light behind the tree to shine through the holes! So pretty.

# ADVENT CALENDAR TREE

Although I love this paper pocket Advent calendar tree, you can adapt it to suit your space and decor. For example, string up your paper pockets like a garland, hang from an actual tree, bunch them up or tape them to the wall in the shape of a Christmas tree. The choice is yours. As this craft uses gift wrap, it will match your Christmas color schemes. It can also be made in plain colors or just brown kraft paper.

## MATERIALS

- Scraps of Christmas gift wrap*
- Brown kraft paper
- Baker's twine or ribbons
- Small gifts

  *Any paper would work just fine, too!

## TOOLS

- Lead pencil
- Scissors
- Stapler
- Pens (optional)

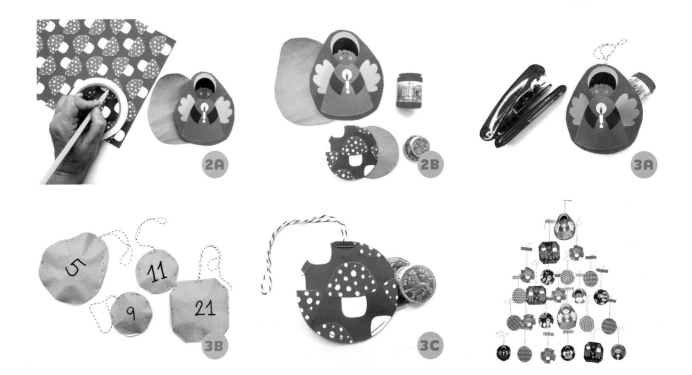

1. See how many kinds of different patterned or colored paper you can find—anything goes: gift wrap, printed paper . . . Or you can make this out of brown paper and stick on red paper hearts, or use white paper and add stripes and spots with pens! Make the most of what you have!

2. Use anything for tracing a circle and trace lots of circles, keeping the patterns on the paper in mind. For example, if there is an angel, make sure it's facing the right way up and that you don't cut a leg off! You can also cut shapes or follow the shape of your pattern. Lay over some brown kraft paper and cut out both pieces at the same time so that they match.

3. Staple some baker's twine in place to serve as hangers, again being mindful of any patterns. The baker's twine should go at the top of any picture or pattern. Staple all the way round—leaving a gap for your gift. Then, add your gift and staple shut. Add a number from 1 to 24 in pen on the back, if you wish! Repeat until you have 24 gifts all packaged up and ready to hang.

## DISPLAY OPTIONS

1. A tree with all-brown numbers facing forward: Turn each number in order, 1 per day, through Advent to reveal the tree. Remove the gifts carefully and leave the decoration up! The tree can go on a plain wall or the back of a door.

2. A tree with the brown numbers facing backward: Carefully seek and find the right number for each day.

3. A garland: Run a ribbon or fairy lights through all the gifts and hang across a mantelpiece, shelf or windowsill.

4. On a tree: Hang as ornaments—you can use large twigs from the garden or a real Christmas tree.

5. Attach all your mini wrapped packages to a cardboard hoop and turn it into a wreath!

# DIY
# SANTA GIFT BAGS

Do you have an awkwardly shaped gift? Or something small you need to wrap in a hurry? These paper gift bags are so easy to make, and can be made in any size—from small (use printer paper) to large (use wrapping paper or brown kraft paper). Then decorate to personalize and make really fun! Today's decorations are all about Christmas, but I am sure you can find some design inspiration in this book to turn this easy paper craft into something for Halloween or Easter, too!

## MATERIALS

- 1 sheet of paper, 5½" x 8½" or A5 (14.8 x 21 cm) or as needed for gift
- Scraps of contrasting paper

## TOOLS

- Tape
- Ruler
- Scissors (optional)
- Pens (optional)
- Glue stick (optional)

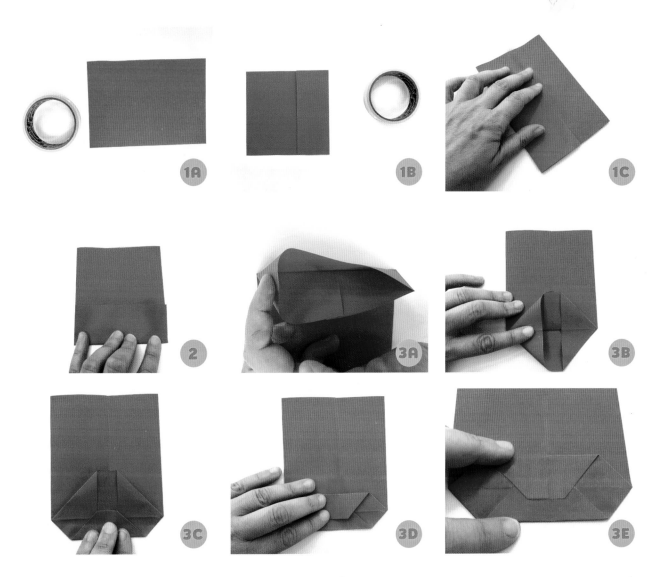

1. Lay the paper in front of you with the long side parallel to you. Fold the right-hand edge toward the left, to just over the halfway point. Then, take the left-hand edge and repeat. Secure with some tape. This will roughly be the width of your paper gift bag.

2. Now, make the base of your gift bag. Fold the bottom of your paper upward—in this case I folded it by about 1½ inches (4 cm). But you can make it thinner (e.g., for a chocolate bar) or wider (e.g., for a teddy bear). This will determine the depth of your gift bag.

3. Take the corner of the lifted flap and push it in to create a triangle. Repeat on the other side, then press them flat. Make another little flap that folds just over midway. And repeat from the top. Secure with tape. Your basic paper gift bag is now complete. You can fill it and tape it down!

(continued)

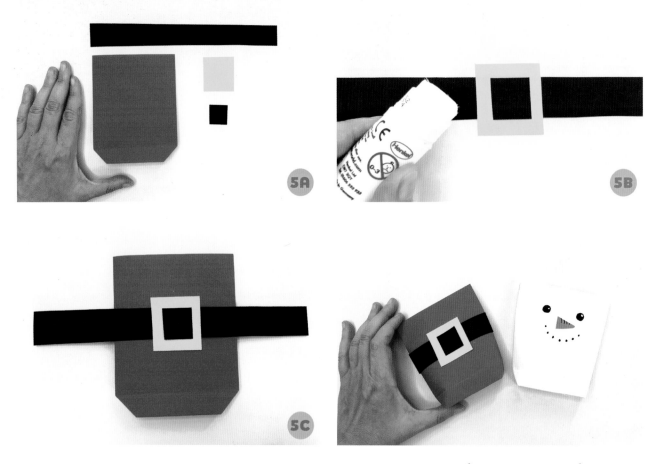

# DIY SANTA GIFT BAGS (CONT.)

## FOR A SNOWMAN

4. Use white paper for the bag. Just add details in pen and a piece of orange paper for the nose.

## FOR A SANTA CLAUS

5. Use red paper for the bag. Cut a strip of long black paper, a black square (the same width as the strip) and a large yellow square. Glue the small black square into the yellow square and then onto the black strip. Secure onto the gift bag.

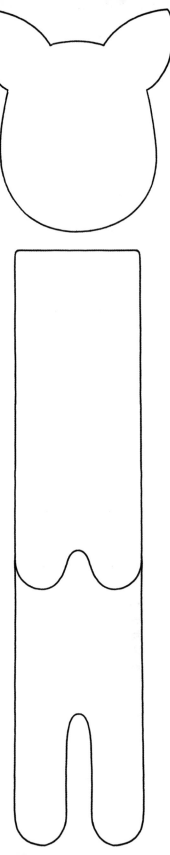
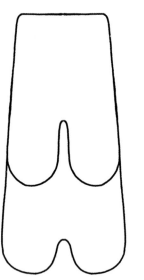

# TEMPLATES

## UNICORN & PANDACORN
## "HUG A BOOK" (PAGE 20)

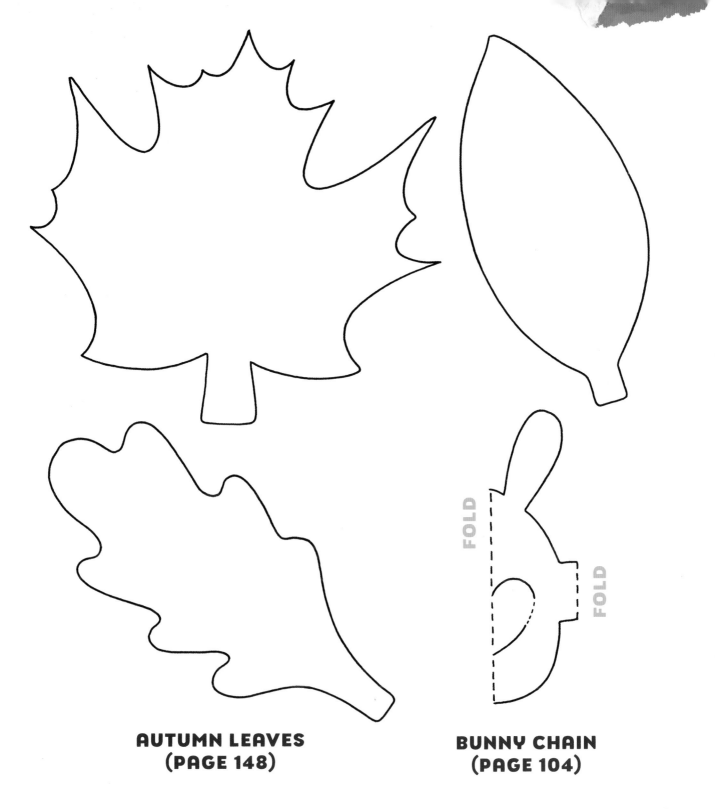

**AUTUMN LEAVES
(PAGE 148)**

**BUNNY CHAIN
(PAGE 104)**

FOLD

FOLD

**KIRIGAMI BUTTERFLY (PAGE 138)**

**GINGERBREAD CARDS (PAGE 166)**

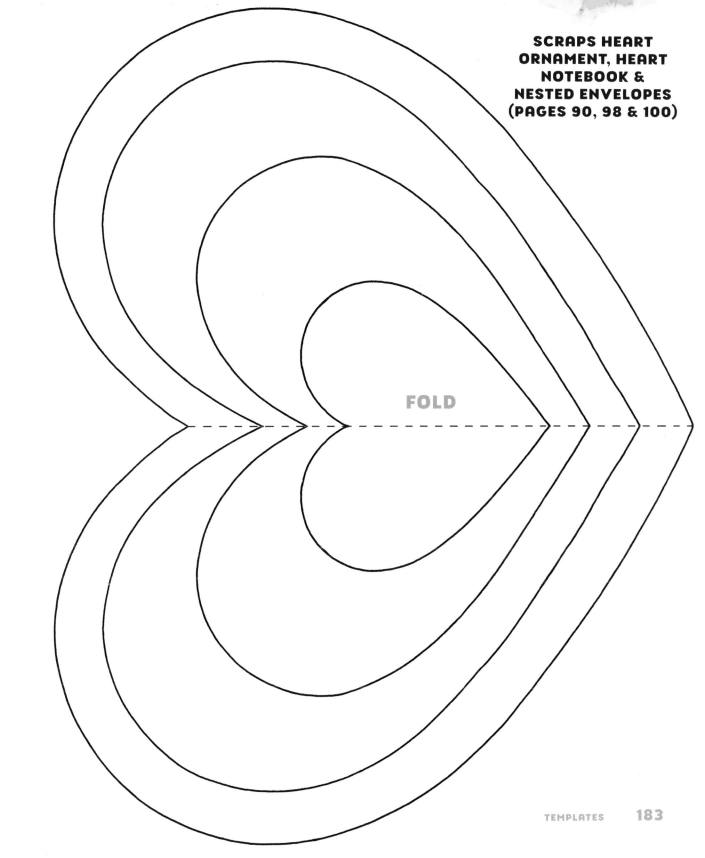

SCRAPS HEART
ORNAMENT, HEART
NOTEBOOK &
NESTED ENVELOPES
(PAGES 90, 98 & 100)

FOLD

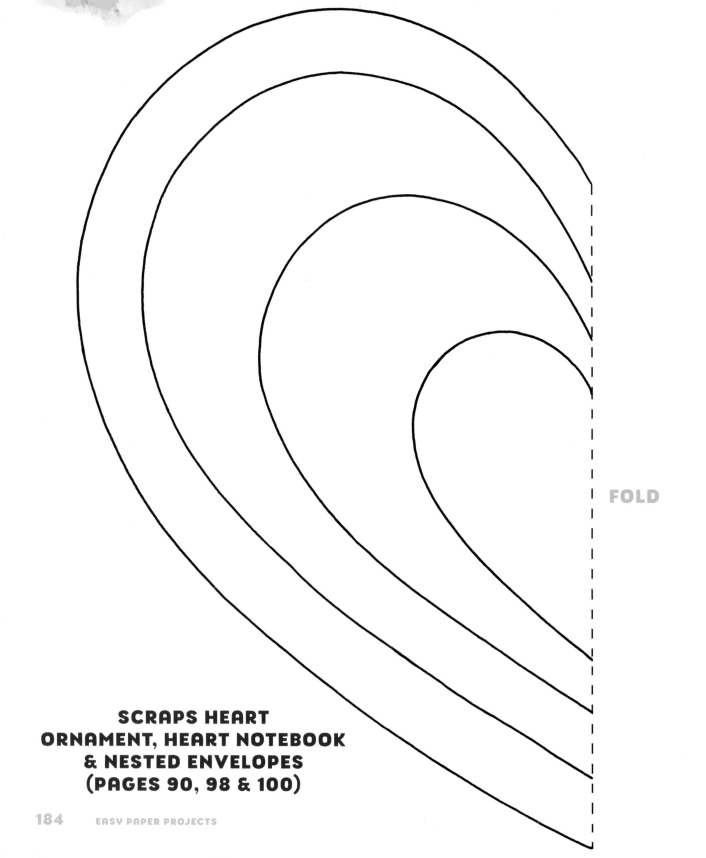

FOLD

**SCRAPS HEART
ORNAMENT, HEART NOTEBOOK
& NESTED ENVELOPES
(PAGES 90, 98 & 100)**

# ACKNOWLEDGMENTS

Some crafts in this book have been influenced by my Red Ted Art readers; for instance, the Paper Angels in this book (page 168) were originally made using a wooden bead. The angels in this book have a cute paper face and hair, thanks to a reader sending in her lovely photos and giving me permission to use her design here. Please do send me photos of your creations! I love to see them.

I would also like to thank Emma, Ana, Manja and Isabelle for joining me on this book-writing journey, frequently listening to my inspirational woes, advising me on photography and simply being there and routing for me! You guys rock!

A big thank-you for the team at Page Street! You turned my rambling creative ideas into this beautiful, well-organized and laid-out book.

Finally, I have to thank Celia, once again, for her years of creative encouragement and support!

# ABOUT THE AUTHOR

## OH, HOW I LOVE TO CRAFT.

I have been a craft enthusiast all my life. I have early childhood memories of sitting in a warm cozy kitchen in early winter and crafting for Christmas. Making a Santa from walnuts and oranges (yes, it is possible . . .) and pine cone owls. Painting eggs at Easter and then making cat decorations at school for Halloween.

When I was in my early teens, my adoptive grandmother, Celia, taught me how to knit and sew and encouraged and nurtured all my crafty activities. It was all about having a go, learning, experimenting and trying out new things.

Then, I grew up. Life and work got in the way, but I always kept my love for crafting going—with homemade birthday cards and small homemade gifts at Christmas.

Once my children were born, I found the time to go back to my childhood memories and start a new legacy of crafting with them. I started my website RedTedArt.com about nine years ago and my YouTube channel four years ago. My children (now 11 and 9 years old), my online readers and, on occasion, the kids at my children's school have given me lots of opportunities to craft with children of all ages—and learn lots about what works and what doesn't work and how kids like to craft! I am super keen to help share skills and techniques for readers to then turn into their own creations.

In 2013, I published my first book, *Red Ted Art: Cute and Easy Crafts for Kids*, which was an eclectic mix of "best crafts" from the website at the time. I am excited about this new paper crafts book, which is more focused and builds on my knowledge gained since. This book has been written with you in mind. I hope you like it as much as I do!

# INDEX